IN THE BALANCE

CHRIST 7 WEIGHS *the* HEARTS *of* CHURCHES

~ BY ALLEN SATTERLEE ~

CREST BOOKS

Salvation Army National Headquarters
Alexandria, VA, USA

Published by Crest Books
The Salvation Army National Headquarters
615 Slaters Lane, Alexandria, VA 22313
Phone: 703 / 684-5523
Fax: 703 / 302-8617

Major Allen Satterlee – Editor in Chief and National Literary Secretary
Judith L. Brown – Crest Books Editor
Roger O. Selvage Jr. – Art Director
Henry Cao – Graphic Designer

Available from The Salvation Army Supplies and Purchasing Departments
> Des Plaines, IL – (847) 937-8896
> West Nyack, NY – (888) 488-4882
> Atlanta, GA – (800) 786-7372
> Long Beach, CA – (847) 937-8896

Or visit www.shop.salvationarmy.org

ISBN: 978-0-9831482-9-6
Library of Congress Control Number: 2013945139

Other books by Allen Satterlee:
Determined to Conquer: The History of The Salvation Army Caribbean Territory; Voices from Haiti; Salvation Assault: The History of The Salvation Army in Papua New Guinea; Turning Points: How The Salvation Army Found a Different Path; Sweeping Through the Land: The History of The Salvation Army in the Southern United States; Notable Quotables: A Compendium of Gems from Salvation Army Literature

Cover Illustration:
The Victorious Lion Of Judah by C. Michael Dudash
Mission House Artworks, www.cmdudash.com

Photo Credits on the following pages:
iStock Photo: xv, 7, 9, 12, 17, 37, 45, 69, 70, 86, 124,129; Hemera: 6; Innogames GmbH: 3; Ken Fairfax: 24; Marie–Lan Nguyen: 38; Gregory White: 29; Wikimedia Commons: 31, 32, 64, 121; Neru Kenji: 48; Aleksandra Yevteyeva: 53, Patrick Taylor: 58; Rena Hampton: 75; Ben Marsh: 83; Paolo Giocoso: 91; Cristina David: 100; Francesco Hayez: 105; Stella M.: 108

Cartography Credits on the following pages:
xx, 22, 42, 62, 80, 98, 118; Map Design, Roger Selvage, Salvation Army NHQ Publication Dept.; Lambert Conformal Conic Projection, CIA World Fact Book

CONTENTS

IN THE BALANCE

PREFACE

The final book in the canon—traditionally referred to as "The Revelation of St. John the Divine"—has caused considerable discussion and angst among those who wish to study it, be they serious scholar or faithful reader. It is unlike the rest of the New Testament.

But while many of the chapters of Revelation are subject to analysis, difference of opinion and understanding, which indeed at times has been contentious, the subject of the material that follows certainly is not. Our attention is carefully drawn to the letters written to seven churches in ancient Asia Minor, which Allen Satterlee carefully examines, sensitively explicates, and prophetically presents.

The book is not just a scholarly treatise, although it does show evidence of serious study; let me suggest, rather, it is primarily a pastoral communication. It demonstrates clarity of purpose, and is irenic in nature. It is a presentation of the Gospel message, thoroughly grounded in Holy Scripture.

The chapters deal with each of the seven churches, as portrayed in the letters addressed to each one, concerning their relationship to their Lord and the need to be faithful to Him. The author correctly notes that while each of the seven Christian communities receives its own message, they are to read what is said to the others. The subjects differ, but each announces the need for spiritual soundness and freedom from heresy within the church.

William Barclay, eminent preacher and recent Biblical commentator, notes that Revelation "is infinitely worth studying, for it contains the blazing faith of the Christian Church in the days when life was an agony … but still believed that beyond the terror was the glory and above the raging of men was the power of God."

The prayer of the author, indeed mine as well, is that as these pages are read and the lessons are learned, the Spirit of God will make them come alive in our own lives, all to His honor and glory. I am privileged to commend it to your reading, which I do so without reservation.

Commissioner William A. Roberts
USA National Commander

ACKNOWLEDGEMENTS

Although I might have been able to write this book without any help from others, to do so would have been infinitely more difficult and very frustrating. I am deeply grateful for those who have helped me along the way. My wife, Esther, has been there when the idea for each of my books moves from my silent brooding through to the up and down path to publication. I appreciate her support and belief in my writing ministry.

I am very fortunate that I have been given not only great cooperation but active support and means from The Salvation Army, which not only serves as my spiritual home but the avenue for my full time calling as a Salvation Army officer. I am particularly grateful to the leaders who allowed me time and backed my writing efforts. Commissioner William A. Roberts, the USA National Commander as well as Colonel William Harfoot, USA National Chief Secretary, were wonderful. I also need to say a special thanks to Mrs. Melissa Hollinger, my administrative assistant, who spent hours and hours helping me with the typing and organizing my notes.

Three individuals agreed to review and then gave valuable feedback on the manuscript. Their remarks helped me see the weaknesses and blind spots, brought to my attention the awkward sentences and faulty logic. So I thank each of these for correcting with grace: Colonel Brian Tuck, Lt. Colonel Marlene Chase and Major Frank Duracher.

Above all, I thank God for the Bible, His inspired text that over twenty centuries has challenged, inspired, informed and transformed those who read it. And I thank Him for His help in writing this book. If there is error, it is wholly mine for lacking the wherewithal to see what He tried to show to me. In the writing of this book, I had to consider what the messages to the churches not only said to the world at large but listen to how they spoke to my life. I am richer for it.

INTRODUCTION

L ike a peninsula connected to a great continent, the letters to the seven churches jut out, both distinct in their form and content as well as clearly and wholly connected to the book of Revelation. The letters are perfectly consistent with the rest of the book, heralding the themes that will follow. But because of their unique character, they can be studied independently to great benefit. In many ways they offer subject matter easier to grasp than much of the cryptic content of Revelation that has left itself open to centuries of speculative interpretation. Whereas a reader may not be able to comprehend all that is intended with the two witnesses, the false prophet, the beast, the great whore or the battle of Armageddon, he can understand a small, persecuted church that is clinging faithfully to the glorified Christ who knows its situation and deeply cherishes it.

The Seven Churches

The seven churches were located in what is now modern Turkey, then the Roman province of Asia. Tracing them on a map will show that they form a rough oval standing on end with a slight tilt westward, beginning with Ephesus and ending with Laodicea. A messenger in that day who sought to visit each church would very likely have followed the track that is laid out in the order that the churches are mentioned. The seven churches seemed to have been linked together in a common identity, much like an administrative district or division. However, there does not seem to have been a headquarters that provided any kind of supervision over them. Because John lived in Ephesus, he would have known each one intimately. Even if he did not exercise ecclesiastical authority over the churches, his apostolic position would have given him considerable influence.

The book of Revelation makes frequent use of numbers to underscore ideas. Seven, the perfect number, represents completeness. That idea of wholeness needs to be kept in mind as well as the fact that the letters were not confidential notes but open communications for all eyes to see. Although there are seven distinct letters, it is not to be imagined that the individual churches read and focused only on their letter to the exclusion of the others. The letters would have been read together as a group in each of the seven congregations so that the Ephesians would have heard what was said to the Smyrneans, the Laodiceans what was said to the Philadelphians. Each would be encouraged and admonished by the content of the messages to the other six while heeding in particular what was said to their own congregation. Further, as the book of Revelation made its way around the Christian world, the seven messages were broadcast, understood and applied to the various local situations. As Christian history unfolded, the content continually was applied as it is even to the present day.

Noteworthy in Christ's selection of these seven churches out of the literally hundreds or even thousands of churches that were interspersed throughout the Roman Empire at this time, is that He did not choose the ones most famous or prominent. There is no mention of Rome or Antioch, Athens or Alexandria. Although among the seven there were cities that were significant in size and influence, there were also ones that would hardly be noticed were they not part of this group.

Absent as well is any direct comment on politics, social causes, cultural shifts or record of even as cataclysmic an event as the fall of Jerusalem in 70 AD. Along this line, William Evans, Presbyterian evangelist of the early twentieth century, notes, "Christ's interests are on the earth and among His churches. It is not in the great governments or massive world movements, it not in the armies and navies of earth, it not with the great capitals of earth that Jesus' interest centers: it is His church."[1]

In addressing the seven churches, Christ spoke about the types of problems that the Church as a body faced in their day. But the truths defined were not only identifiable in these individual circumstances, but in a broader sense across time and geography. The tepid nature

---

[1]William Evans, Christ's Last Message to the Church. 27

of Laodicea has never been purged from the Church as a whole, always existing somewhere. The need for faithful believers to hold on despite the forces gathered against them has continued unabated in all centuries and in a variety of settings as it did in Smyrna in the first century. Just as the messages of the letters were not meant to be read or understood apart from each other among the seven churches, the message of these letters is relevant to the Church two thousand years later. The names of the battlefields may have changed, but there has been no cease-fire in the war.

Religious Challenges to Christianity in the Roman Empire

It is generally accepted that Revelation was written around 95 A.D. by the Apostle John. Christianity was growing at a rate that alarmed both the Roman authorities and the older, well-entrenched traditional Jewish religion. It was also posing a major threat to the various polytheistic religions and their variations. For example, although the riot in Ephesus over the worship of Artemis recorded in Acts 19 would have occurred a generation earlier then when Revelation was written, the incident was hardly forgotten.

The religious climate in ancient Rome was anything but unified. The Roman government allowed considerable latitude for conquered people to maintain and practice their religious beliefs as long as they were not at odds with the goals of the Empire. With the intricate and well operating system of roads and free navigation of the Mediterranean, ethnic and national groups intermingled as never before in history. With the contact came cross-pollination of craftsmanship, cultures, philosophies and of course, religions.

While many adhered faithfully to their culture's historic beliefs, there was also a marked tendency to integrate differing religions to a greater or smaller degree with each other. Local gods and goddesses were often absorbed into larger religions that commonly had a counterpart to the local deity. Worship practices in a similar way were adapted or enlarged to encompass the new influences. Rarely was this done with forethought or stated intention. Rather, it was an evolution of ideas.

Other times, there was a deliberate attempt to reconcile differing religions by finding common ground or parallels. Syncretism, the integration of differing religions and their practices, was a reality that caused not only deep concern to the early Christian leaders but has remained a constant menace to Christianity ever since. It is not only because the Scriptures are twisted to meanings never intended or that doctrine is diluted. But the merging of non-Christian thoughts into Christian theology and practices leads to a disintegration of *Christ-like* living and confusion rather than clarity.

The one religion that largely avoided syncretism was Judaism. The Jews' insistence that there was only one God had no corollary in any of the other religions of that day. Adding to that, the Jews' were notoriously racist, clinging tenaciously to their claim to be God's chosen people, even as they existed as communities within larger communities—among the very ones they considered their inferiors. While there were isolated incidences of syncretism in Jewish practice, it was usually rooted out whenever it was found. During the intertestamental period the heroic struggles of the Maccabees not only recorded historic action against syncretism but also served as warning to those who would compromise.

When Christianity entered the scene, its outreach crossed the bridge between Judaism and the Gentile world. The first Christians were almost entirely Jewish but as the religion spread beyond the borders of what had been the nation of Israel, the balance tipped in favor of Gentile believers. What began as a trickle became a flood, leaving Jewish believers hugely outnumbered. Most of these Gentile believers had known little or nothing of Judaism, its Scriptures, worship or ceremony prior to their conversion and so the transition to Christianity was not as easy. The concept of monotheism was difficult enough but more challenging teachings of Christianity were even thornier. The nature of Christ as fully God and fully man fit into no previous framework to make the doctrine easier to digest. Added to that was the belief in the Trinity that spoke of three as one while insisting that it was not another brand of polytheism. The emerging New Testament and other Christian writings had to be weighed against those of the Old Testament as well as their faithfulness to the Apostles' teaching.

Part of the answer, at least to some, was to water down the more prickly issues of Christianity, both teaching and practice. Heresies that sought to alter the fundamentals of the Faith were constantly cropping up; usually led by a charismatic leader and which on the surface had teachings that were somewhat palatable with some orthodox belief. Defining their error had a mutual benefit of fighting false doctrine but also clarifying orthodox Christian belief.

Other attempts included grafting in the teachings of other religions to form a hybrid of sorts that allowed the believer to keep some of the old beliefs. With the teachings also came the moral imperatives or lack thereof. Some beliefs of other religions did indeed have a parallel in Christianity, again forcing the believers to carefully weigh and then bring answers to people who needed to understand with their heads as much as believe in their hearts.

It was a turbulent period made so by the constant addition of believers who needed instruction and discipling in how to live, the pull of heresies that threatened to undermine the gospel with additions, deletions or unexpected twists, and the growing opposition of the Jewish community to this upstart religion that claimed to have fulfilled what they had guarded through the centuries. Added to that was the growing opposition of the mighty Roman Empire that actively fought to exterminate the Christian religion and its followers.

The Role of Persecution

Persecution was the favorite tool of the Roman authorities for nearly two and a half centuries in battling Christianity. With absolute power over the lives of the people in the Empire, coupled with its system of laws and courts, it was not difficult to pass and enforce legislation that made criminals out of those who followed Christ. Beyond that, the Emperor exercised wide-ranging power outside of the legislative process. If he deemed anyone or anything a threat or an annoyance, his disapproval could be expressed and enforced with the might of the Empire. As Christianity grew and battle lines were more clearly drawn, persecution became more widespread, organized and severe. There were lulls from time to time, welcome respites to those targeted. In addition, the persecutions varied in their brutality from one part of the Empire to the other. While some Christians endured withering fire from the enemy, others were allowed to have periods of peace. However, no matter where they were, the specter of persecution always was there, regardless of any calm in the moment. No Christian could afford to breathe easy.

Christians suffered sporadic persecution under the Jewish leaders in Palestine, initiated by the crucifixion of Christ. Spontaneous persecution arose as Christianity spread in the form of riots, harassment and social isolation. The first Roman persecution of Christians was under Nero, one that was particularly cruel at the hands of a sadistic and criminally insane despot. It did not last long nor was it very extensive, manifested almost entirely in the environs surrounding the city of Rome.

Domitian was responsible for the first Empire wide persecution. With the Christians refusing to bow down at his temples, he interpreted their defiance as an act of treason. He likely had no particular interest in the content of Christian belief itself, caring only that they rebelled against an oath of loyalty under religious guise. With many restive peoples under Roman rule, such disloyalty could not be tolerated. His persecution intended the dual purpose of dealing with the criminal actions of the Christians while also serving as an example to any who would refuse to bend the knee to him. But persecuting Christians was sometimes done even while giving them grudging admiration. Emperor Hadrian sent out one of his men, Aristides, to infiltrate and report back on the Christians. His report about them must have caused pause in the Roman court: "Behold! How they love one another!"

John on Patmos

It was under Domitian that John the Apostle was banished to the insignificant Mediterranean island of Patmos. The island is a rocky, difficult place with no natural source for water other than catching

The Apostle John was banished to the Mediterranean island of Patmos as an enemy of the state. After the emperor Domitian died he was allowed to return home to Ephesus.

Christ Weighs the Hearts of 7 Churches

the rain. It was a fitting place for punishment. Banning enemies of the state to such places was common practice in ancient times. It might be that John was banished there instead of being outright martyred in deference to his advanced age, which at this time would have made him around 85-90 years old. But it was hardly a reprieve.

To be banished in this way involved more than being exiled from friends and family. A number of the prisoner's rights vanished including the loss of his personal property. When he died, all his possessions that might remain were taken by Rome. The prisoner knew that when he stepped foot on the island it would be the last place he would see on earth. There was no chance he could ever return home. Although a small living allowance was given to him and he was free to move around the island, he could not correspond with or receive correspondence from anyone in the outside world. The modern equivalent is found in Siberia, where the Russian government while under czarist and communist rule, exiled millions in what became a grinding down until only the last breath remained to be taken.

John's banishment was even more severe than what normally was endured. Preceded by a severe scourging, John would have been kept in shackles, poorly fed and clothed, left to sleep on a cold stone floor and sent to hard labor under the cruel whip of a Roman overseer. Given his age, the suffering for John must have been particularly difficult to endure. Surely no one expected him to last very long. It would be a martyrdom with no glory, no Christians taking courage from watching the last of Jesus' original Twelve standing true to his faith.

In this most hopeless of situations and most desolate of places, John not only endured but also was in the place and situation where God could reveal to him the vision of Revelation. Sir William Ramsay, Scottish archaeologist and New Testament scholar of the early twentieth century, pays tribute by saying, "In that living death he found his true life, like many another martyr of Christ. Who shall tell how far a man may rise above earth, when he can rise superior to an environment like that? Who will set the bounds to the growth of the human soul, when it is separated from all worldly relations and trammels, feeding on its own thoughts and the divine nature, and yet is filled not with anxiety about its poor self, but with care, love and sympathy for those who have constituted its charge?"[2]

That might have been where John ended his life but for Domitian's fate, one shared by many tyrants throughout history. Assassinated by court officials, after his death the Roman Senate sought to erase any memory of him. His statues were destroyed, his name removed from buildings and his edicts reversed. This included those banished by him, resulting in John being allowed to leave Patmos to return to his home in Ephesus. With Domitian's death there was a short break in the imperial persecutions.

Interpretation of the Seven Letters

This study of the seven churches focuses on them in their historic setting at the end of the first century. No symbolism is seen in the Scriptures regarding these churches other than what is intended, i.e., tree of life, white robes, etc.

Some have seen the seven churches representing the seven ages of the Church. While that has some appeal and indeed there are parallels to what was happening in the churches to periods of history, there are serious flaws with this approach as well.

One such flaw is that in this view the first and second churches overlap to represent the first period of Church history and the sixth and seventh churches represent the current history of the church. This seems strange and leaves one to ask, if these two periods had to be articulated through overlapping experiences, why not the other three periods of the Church?

Another more serious flaw is that the historical symbolism fails to take into account what was happening in the Church outside of Protestant Europe and North America. Church history in Asia, Africa and Latin America is totally ignored. The history of the Orthodox Church and Roman Catholic Church (after the Reforma-

---

[2]William Ramsay, The Letters to the Seven Churches. 98

tion) are also overlooked. It may be that the exponents of this view feel that the only true keepers of the Faith are in the Protestant movement. But that is presumptuous at the very least, arrogant at the very worst. Although there are theological differences between the Protestant, Roman Catholic, Orthodox and other branches of Christianity, each has a valid story.

It is doubtful that when Christ gave His word on these churches He was prophesying about the historic ages of the Church or that if He was, it was to the exclusion of millions of believers who sincerely and wholeheartedly follow Him.

It is best to read the text for its plain meaning rather than bringing in preconceived notions seeking support for pet beliefs.

Discussion Questions

1. Given the highly personal and sometimes critical content of the letters to the seven churches, how would you feel if a letter like this was written to you and then shared openly with the world?

2. Syncretism has been defined as "the combination of different forms of belief or practice." What examples of syncretism can you think of that affect twenty-first century Christianity?

3. The author says that in fighting against heresies, Christian beliefs were more clearly defined. How is that possible?

4. How is hostility toward Christianity shown presently in our world?

5. Aristides reported on the Christians, "Behold! How they love one another!" What report would Aristides make about Christians based on your church?

IN THE BALANCE

IN THE BALANCE

Personal Reflection

1. Imagine in a moment that you were transported back to the time of the writing of Revelation. How would you face the challenges faced by this generation of Christians?

2. If you were to make a report about your church what would you say? How does your role contribute to this picture?

3. Why do you think the Lord focused on these seven churches in this small area of the world?

4. If you were exiled like John with no hope of ever returning home, given your current spiritual life, would you have enough to sustain you?

Revelation 2:1-7
To the Church in Ephesus

1 "To the angel[a] of the church in Ephesus write:

These are the words of him who holds the seven stars in his right hand and walks among the seven golden lampstands. 2 I know your deeds, your hard work and your perseverance. I know that you cannot tolerate wicked people, that you have tested those who claim to be apostles but are not, and have found them false. 3 You have persevered and have endured hardships for my name, and have not grown weary.

4 Yet I hold this against you: You have forsaken the love you had at first. 5 Consider how far you have fallen! Repent and do the things you did at first. If you do not repent, I will come to you and remove your lampstand from its place. 6 But you have this in your favor: You hate the practices of the Nicolaitans, which I also hate.

7 Whoever has ears, let them hear what the Spirit says to the churches. To the one who is victorious, I will give the right to eat from the tree of life, which is in the paradise of God."

EPHESUS:
Rekindling a Lost Love

— Revelation 2:1-7

While a fugitive from King Saul, David and his men prepared to join the Philistines to go to battle against him. They were sent back, not allowed to fight because they were not trusted, the Philistines fearing that their unproven allies would turn against them in the heat of battle. But upon returning to their camp they found that it had been raided (1 Samuel 30:25). Missing were not only all their possessions but much to their grief, their wives and children as well. They soon gathered themselves to go after what they loved most, riding furiously until they found the raiders, engaging them victoriously in battle to recapture their families. Ironically, when they originally rode out to conquer, they became the victims and nearly lost what mattered most.

The church in Ephesus found itself in the part of the story where they found that what was most precious was missing. What would they do about it?

The Mighty City of Ephesus

In the first century, Ephesus was estimated to be home to between 250,000-400,000 people. It sat squarely at a crossroads that brought trade from the East, the North and the South. Its inland harbor teemed with ships and sailors, goods and merchants. So great was the city of Ephesus that the terms "Asia" and "Ephesus" were synonymous. Because the trade was so active and well known, many scholars feel that the passage in Revelation 18:12-13 is a reference to

EPHESUS: Rekindling a Lost Love

Ephesus where it speaks of "cargoes of gold, silver, precious stones and pearls; fine linen, purple, silk and scarlet cloth; every sort of citron wood, and articles of every kind made of ivory, costly wood, bronze, iron and marble; cargoes of cinnamon and spice, of incense, myrrh and frankincense, of wine and olive oil, of fine flour and wheat; cattle and sheep; horses and carriages; and human beings sold as slaves."

The area had been a major settlement since 6000 B.C., later serving as the capital city of the Ahiyava Kingdom in 3000 B.C.. It changed hands many times, in turn ruled by the Mycenaeans, Karians, Lydians, Persians, Macedonians, Ptolemies, and Seleucids before becoming part of the Roman Empire. The last of the conquerors named it a free city, allowing it self-government without the indignity of a Roman garrison being quartered there.

According to Greek historian Herodotus, the city was named after Ephos, queen of the Amazons, the legendary tribe of fierce female warriors. The name also actually has two very different connotations: "desirable one" and "to let go, to relax."

It was magnificent to behold. The Marble Street was paved with slabs of marble so perfectly fit that even a piece of paper could not breach the seams where the stones were joined. It boasted the Library of Celsus, a repository of records whose ornate steps led to a square of marble and mosaic tiles. There was also the Hall of Tyrannus, a debating center at a time when debating was considered to be not only informative but a form of high entertainment. The Theater of Ephesus could seat upwards to 25,000 people. Lining the streets, along with every major sculpture and relief were to be found depictions of fully armored Roman soldiers, undoubtedly in mind when Paul wrote about the full armor of God in Ephesians 6.

But as great as were these features, nothing matched one of the Seven Wonders of the Ancient World, the Temple of Artemis.

The Temple of Artemis

At a site so ancient that its origins were cloaked in the twilight of antiquity stood the Temple of Artemis (Diana to the Romans).

Temple of Artemis, Diana to the Romans, built by Alexander the Great in 333 B.C.

Legend was that the statue of the goddess had descended from heaven from the hand of Zeus (Acts 19:35). Notwithstanding that claim, prior to the arrival of the Greeks a very similar local goddess named Kubaba was worshipped. Since she bore such a close resemblance to the Greek goddess Artemis, the temple and its myth were easily grafted into the Greek religion.

Over the centuries a series of temples to a female goddess had stood on the spot. Each version was larger and more ornate than its predecessor. An insane man, whose sole purpose in doing so was to make a name for himself, burned down the one that preceded New Testament days. This act was done the night that Alexander the Great was born. Struck by that fact, in 333 B.C. Alexander determined to build a more magnificent temple than had ever existed there. Ancient accounts testify to the success of Alexander's intent. The Greeks lauded it by saying; "The sun sees nothing finer in his course than Diana's temple."

Using the dimensions of the previous temple, it is calculated to have been four times the size of the Acropolis in Athens. It measured 342 feet (104 meters) in length, 164 feet in width (50 meters) with columns that stretched 55 feet (17 meters) high. It covered an area of 100,000 square feet (9300 square meters). The dimensions alone were awe-inspiring but the beauty of the temple was even more so.

Supposedly carved from single stones, there were 127 gleaming white Parian marble columns, 36 of which were overlaid with gold and jewels. The temple area was open with only the center roofed with cedar tiles. Folding doors were carved from the finest cypress. Leading to the roof was a stairway, allegedly cut from a single gigantic vine from the island of Cyprus.

Painted to make them lifelike, statues of gods and goddesses towered over worshippers. The temple housed an incredible collection of art, including four bronze statues of Amazon warriors. The inner shrine boasted a great altar, carved by the greatest of Greek sculptors, Praxiteles. Behind the altar were velvet curtains that cloaked the statue of Artemis. Beyond the statue was yet another inner chamber, a secure stronghold for treasure and wealth, allowing the temple to double as a repository of some of the greatest wealth in the ancient world.

Artemis herself hardly presented an attractive figure. One of the earliest statues of her is described by past president of Bangor Theological Seminary, Kent Ulery: "...big breasted, huge hipped, obscenely obese goddess of nature, arms perched with female lions, squatting to give birth to Attis, the god of vegetation..."[3] A later depiction shows her with rows of breasts, which some believe to actually be the testicles of a herd of bulls. In the temple itself, the statue of Artemis included a chest laden with breasts, as the goddess squatted with a club in one hand and a trident in the other. Artemis was the goddess of the forest, the hunt, as well as serving as the guardian of women's virginity and their protector in childbirth.

Later, as Christianity replaced the old mythology of Greek and

---

[3] Kent Ulery, *No Longer at Ease: Seven Churches and the Empire, a Study in Revelation 1-3. 22*

Rome, Mary worship arose, an act of syncretism that involved many of the rites of Artemis migrating into Christian worship. No doubt this arose because Mary, the mother of Jesus, was supposed to have lived in Ephesus with John. A tomb in the city reportedly is where Mary is buried. The Roman Catholic Church maintains that Mary was assumed into heaven from Ephesus.

Eminent New Testament scholar and commentator William Barclay, shares that the worship of Artemis occurred with "the accompaniments of shouts and wailings, the burning of incense and the playing of the flute …worshippers worked themselves up into an emotional and hysterical frenzy…"[4]

Because Artemis was the god of childbirth, prayers for fertility brought people to the temple. It was believed that by having sexual relations with one of the many temple prostitutes, a couple would be able to conceive themselves. Quite naturally, what was called worship over time degenerated into disgraceful and shameless acts of sexual license, wishes for fertility notwithstanding. This contributed to the Ephesians being known as highly immoral and extremely lax in their sexual fidelity.

Another aspect of the worship at the Temple of Artemis was the granting of "Ephesian letters," essentially lucky charms that could be purchased to magically guarantee a safe journey or a prosperous business venture.

The temple was a sanctuary for anyone seeking safety from his or her enemies. Anyone within a bow's shot of it was protected from arrest or attack. Because of this the temple became a gathering place for criminals. Living near the temple was a risk at best as some lawbreakers headquartered at the temple sallied forth under the cloak of darkness to steal, rape or commit other acts of violence. Many criminals chose to live permanently in the temple, creating a tension between worshippers and those who might intimidate or take advantage of them.

Offerings brought to the temple not only supported its upkeep

---

[4] William Barclay, *Letters to the Seven Churches.* 15

Diana, Roman goddess of the forest, guardian of female virginity and protector in childbirth

but also were used to address the needs of the poor and the traveler. This no doubt provided benefit to the silversmiths put out of business by the rising popularity of Christianity (Acts 19).

After being destroyed by Goth invaders, no trace of the temple could be found until an archaeological expedition in 1869 found what remains of it.

Emperor Worship

A later but important development in the religious life of the Roman Empire was the worship of the Roman emperor. Romans were extremely tolerant of the many religions within their empire but they were deeply concerned about the divisiveness that nationalism and religions could create. Beyond stroking the ego of the Roman leaders, the emperor worship was eventually seen as a common act to tie its entire people together. Regardless of their primary religious beliefs, once a year the people were required to come to the Imperial temple, burn incense, kneel down and say, "Caesar is lord." It is not difficult to understand why Christians, who proclaimed Christ alone as Lord, would stand against this practice.

Initially, the emperors resisted worship of themselves but Domitian relished and eventually demanded it. Ruling the Roman Empire from 51 – 96 A.D., Domitian declared himself lord and god, *"Dominus et Deus."* No one was spared calling him this—not even his wife.

It was a signal honor for a city to be allowed to erect a temple to an individual emperor. The Ephesians were pleased to be allowed to build a temple to Domitian and in doing so, constructed one that if it did not eclipse the Temple of Artemis, stood a close second to it. A massive statue of Domitian was erected, nearly 25 feet

(7.5 meters) high, larger than any other statue of a god in the city.

Domitian commanded the first empire wide persecution of Christians, although this seems to have been restricted largely to confiscation of property and banishment. In the case of John and other prisoners like him, life long banishment to penal islands like Patmos was tantamount to a death sentence because they were never allowed to leave once banished. In addition, conditions were incredibly harsh, making death a welcome respite from a miserable life. While violent deaths of Christians also occurred, they seem to have been more the result of local decisions rather than the expected outcome of arrest by the central Roman government. The real danger to Christianity at this time was not martyrdom—that would soon come —but the compromise of kneeling before Caesar's statue and declaring him lord and to be spared any suffering at all.

Despite having a long and extremely productive reign, court officials assassinated Domitian. Because his rule was brutal he made powerful enemies. Soon after his death the Roman Senate obliterated the memory of Domitian. With that all his acts of punishment were declared null and void and his statues ordered destroyed. It was only because of the Roman Senate's action that John was able to return to Ephesus.

Jewish and Christian Presence in Ephesus

Since the time of Greek rule, a significant Jewish community flourished in Ephesus. Maintaining their distinctive religion and practices, their success as business people and civic leaders elicited a number of concessions granted to them by the Greek government leaders. Such special provisions were not allowed for any other ethnic or religious group. For example, Jews were permitted to observe the Sabbath with no penalties resulting. When the Roman rule began, the concessions were extended, much to the resentment of the other Ephesians. They saw the Jews as favored and, because they refused to acknowledge Artemis or any of the other pantheons of Greek and Roman gods as divine, they were viewed as standing against all that made Ephesus a favored place.

When Christianity arrived, probably through the preaching team of Paul, Aquila and Priscilla, the delicate balance between the Jews and the other Gentile people was threatened. At that time, Christianity was seen as a sect within Judaism. Their aggressive evangelism caused strong reaction. The enemies of the Jews did not bother to distinguish between what the Christians did and the Jews did. They were thrown together as uncomfortable bedmates. For their part, the Jews who did not turn to Christ actively sought to distance themselves from this troublesome offshoot.

Acts 19 outlines the conflict that arose because so many Gentiles turned to Christ that the silversmiths' trade, fueled by crafting images of Artemis, was gravely threatened. Making it a battle of religions rather than a trade issue, a silversmith named Demetrius stirred up opposition that was ensued by a riot. The whole city in an uproar, it was only with great difficulty that order was restored. But the incident underscored to the Gentiles and the Jews that the Christians were not only a force to be reckoned with but that they were not going to follow the accepted rules of a tense but uneasy understanding that was at work in the city.

As sharper distinctions were made between traditional Judaism and Christianity, the Jewish community did not want to see their own privileges extended to the Christians. The large number of Gentile converts meant that much of the Christian following was not Jewish at all. It may have been correctly feared that some held an allegiance to Christianity not out of religious conversion but as a way to get around the rules for everyone who was not Jewish. No doubt many were also concerned that the emerging Christianity disposed of long held Jewish rites such as circumcision and food laws. In their mind, Christianity represented a heretical perversion of their religion.

As opposition arose against the Christians, they found not only offended Gentiles but also Jewish believers standing against them. What helped the Ephesian church stand strong was that the growing number of believers was becoming large enough to wield its own political and economic clout. The strength of the church was evidenced when, following the fall of Jerusalem in 70 A.D., Ephesus became the temporary headquarters for the Christian church.

But the tide would turn against the church. Ignatius later recorded that Ephesus was on the highway of the martyrs, "the passage way of those who are slain unto God." From the port of Ephesus the Christians began their journey to Rome, to the Coliseum or death in countless other ways.

This is the crucible that was Ephesus.

Christ Identifies Himself

"To the angel of the church in Ephesus write: These are the words of Him who holds the seven stars in His right hand and walks among the seven golden lamp stands" (Revelation 2:1).

Each of the letters to the churches is addressed to an angel.

The Library of Celsus, where records were kept, had ornate steps leading to a square of marble and mosaic tiles.

Not surprisingly, there is a very wide diversity of opinion as to what is meant by an angel.

1. **Some think that it is a literal angel being addressed, believing that each church has a guardian angel.** The term "angel" is used 60 times in the book of Revelation alone and in each instance means a supernatural or spiritual being. The question is, why would Christ need to address a heavenly being? He could easily do without John being the intermediary. Further, the message is aimed for the church to heed, not an angel to obey, so this doesn't seem to be the answer.

2. **Another explanation, and the one most widely held, is that the angel is the local leader of the church.** The literal meaning of the word angel is "messenger" so that would seem to fit as another term for the one who acted as pastor in these congregations. But the problem is that nowhere in the New Testament does "angel" ever refer to a human. Rather, it is used exclusively for heavenly beings.

3. **A third position is that it is used a collective term for the whole congregation.** Clearly the message is for the congregation of a given church but again, there is no instance in the New Testament for such usage for the term angel.

It is not important to come to some definite conclusion in the matter. The Bible leaves us with tantalizing mysteries like this. Apparently it was clear to John and to the receiving churches what was meant. And, just as clearly, the messages were meant for that specific congregation as a collective group of God's people, not for a heavenly being or an earthly leader to the exclusion of the church. The lamp stands are universally understood as the churches themselves. This is consistent with Jesus' words that His followers were the "light of the world" (Matthew 5:14). The picture of the lamp stand in mind was a menorah, the nine-branch candlestick used in Jewish worship from the time of the Temple. It represented God's faithfulness.

Jesus held or more correctly, cupped, the seven stars in His right hand. The right hand in ancient days was the place of trust and honor. Holding the churches in His right hand, while walking among the lamp stands showed that He was not far off, like the supposed emperor god Domitian who was in Rome. Christ remained near at hand, among His people. That means He knows us and our surroundings, knows our best and worst intentions, our fears and our victories. He is not fooled by secrecy nor does what we do baffle Him. He knows where we are and where we need to be.

"I know your deeds, your hard work and your perseverance. I know that you cannot tolerate wicked people, that you have tested those who claim to be apostles but are not, and have found them false. You have persevered and have endured hardships for my name, and have not grown weary" (Revelation 2:2, 3).

Jesus began with words of commendation. This was a church that had a lot going for it. Their deeds were praiseworthy. The Lord is not citing individual acts as much as a lifestyle of consistent action. Jesus spoke of their hard work, the Greek term meaning backbreaking labor, exhausting work. Jesus also spoke of their perseverance, which could also be translated "triumphant fortitude."[5] These were people who did not roll up their sleeves on a special workday but who showed up every day to tackle what lay before them.

Unlike the present atmosphere in the Western world where people are called on to tolerate any and every aberration of belief and teaching, Jesus commended the Ephesians for what they did *not* tolerate. Jesus recognized that there is always a gravitational pull to

---

[5]*Barclay, 20*

After the fall of Jerusalem in 70 A.D., Ephesus became the temporary headquarters for the Christian church.

lower the high standards of the Christian faith. There are always reasons why compromise seems the best course, when surrendering ground might seem better than fighting a battle alone or quitting the field a wiser course when shot and shell come dangerously close. While compromise is not wrong in itself, it can be when principle is at stake. In that case it can be another word for abdication. It becomes so when we are willing to wink at sin to accommodate actions or a lifestyle that contradicts the teaching of Scripture. The Ephesians are commended for their single-mindedness in standing for the faith against "wicked people." So outstanding was their position that later Ignatius said to the Ephesians, "I ought to be trained for the contest by you ...(for) no heresy has a home among you. No, you do not so much as listen to anyone who speaks of ought else save concerning Jesus Christ in truth ...I have learned that certain people passed through you from Syria bringing evil doctrine, whom you suffered not to sow seed in you, for you stopped your ears."[6]

They stood firm despite the abuse that was heaped upon them. They were ever on guard against false teaching, likely having seen the damage it did elsewhere and recognizing that they, too, could fall victim. But any virtue, it if is not tempered with other graces,

[6]*Quoted in Ulery, 28*

can lead to excess. Constant fighting can make people calloused, looking for enemies when there are none, intolerant of any whose views, allegiance or commitment is perceived to be less than theirs. The diligence of the Ephesians had come at a cost.

Yet I hold this against you: You have forsaken the love you had at first. Consider how far you have fallen! Repent and do the things you did at first. If you do not repent, I will come to you and remove your lamp stand from its place (Revelation 2:4, 5).

Despite the good that they had done and the spirit that kept them in the fight, an essential element was missing. The rebuke stung. "You have forsaken the love you had at first." Like David and his men who had lost what they loved best while off to fight a battle, the Ephesians had lost that which they should have cherished most. In saying this, Jesus used a strong term: forsaken. The Greek word is *aphemi*, meaning to "let go, send away, leave, give up, abandon."[7] This was not a mere bump in the road, a slight deviation off course, a momentary slip in an otherwise exemplary life. This was a turn in a direction away from the destination, a pivot on the heel to turn and deliberately walk away. They had taken up the battle against the evil among them but in doing so had grown deaf to the Commander of the Army of the Lord.

The notorious period of Church history called the Inquisition lasted for nearly seven centuries. Originally it began as an effort by the Church to purify itself of heretical teachings. What began well soon took a terrible turn as the zeal of the inquisitors caused the original purpose to be obscured. Any who thought differently or honestly questioned practices and beliefs of the Church were branded enemies, forced to renounce their stances or face punishment. Over time the penalties became harsher so that even death was not enough. The one considered apostate must suffer as well, resulting in exquisite tools of torture being devised. The righteous

---

[7] *Beacon Bible Commentary*, 494

fervor that energized the inquisitors too often masked villains guilty of far greater crimes of heart than the offenders they were allegedly bringing to justice. Misplaced zeal led to further excesses, as one inquisitor would frequently prove more brutal than his fellow to show his greater devotion to the truth. The Inquisition gave truth to the old proverb that says, "Zeal is like fire; it needs both feeding and watching."

Was there a spirit like that in Ephesus? What exactly had happened? Had they quit loving Christ? Quit loving His people? Both?

It started as coldness in their love for Christ Himself. There was a day when they greeted the morning with praise for their God, when songs of love for Him flowed easily from their lips, a time when they were asked if they were believers, they could feel the joy bubble up as it overflowed into their words of testimony. But that was all routine now. They sang about love even as they thought of other things. They spoke about their allegiance to Christ as they committed unloving acts in His name. Those early days of hallelujah living had settled into dusty doctrinal loyalty that while saying all the right things left them and those around them with a bone-chilling shiver. The famed Anglican cleric, John Stott, has said, "Toil becomes drudgery if it not a labor of love."[8]

An old Salvation Army song asks poignant questions:

Am I what once I was?
Have I that ground maintained
Wherein I walked in power with Thee,
And Thou my soul sustained?

While I speak to Thee,
Lord, Thy goodness show,
Am I what I ought to be?
O Savior, let me know.
— Herbert Booth

---

[8]*Stott, 29*

The Ephesians never really quit loving Christ. But they loved Him less than they did before. They had settled for good instead of best. They were not less orthodox in their belief, but in believing the right things they kept them isolated from the behavior of their daily lives. Their love for Christ cooled from a bright flame to a smoldering ember. The truths are glorious and they bring glory. But this had been lost along the way.

Was it the loss of love for others? The early church fathers felt that this was so, shown by a lack of care for the poor among them. Could it be that the temple of Artemis showed more compassion toward the poverty stricken Christians than the Christians were showing among themselves? Was that not the indictments of the priest and Levite in the story of the Good Samaritan? One reason love is so difficult to define is that it was never meant to be framed by words that prove inadequate but actions that give it flesh.

Perhaps in their defense of the Faith, their words toward each other had become sharper, the grudges more ingrained, the arguments about a point of belief degenerating into a brooding resentment against a brother or sister in Christ. It could just as well be that the division between believers who held different beliefs was so sharp that it had poured into a contemptuous hate. But hate is poor glue because it eventually dissolves what it sticks to.

No doubt it was a combination of both. To despise our brother or sister is to poison our love for God. To cool in our fervor for our Savior inevitably results in a distancing from other people. Sam Storms, author and lead pastor of Bridgeway Church in Oklahoma City, Oklahoma, observes, "Where love for God wanes, love for man diminishes, and where love for man is soured, love for God degenerates into religious formalism, and both constitute a denial of the revelation of God in Christ. If the price paid by the Ephesians for the preservation of true Christianity was the loss of love, the price was too high, for Christianity without love is perverted faith. What we see in the church at Ephesus, therefore, was how their desire for orthodoxy and the exclusion of error had created a climate of suspicion and mistrust in which brotherly love could no longer flourish."[9]

The situation was intolerable. Christ wasted no time demanding a response.

Remember! Repent! Do!
The Ephesian Church was ordered to repent. What constituted true repentance?

1. **Jesus ordered them to remember and keep on remembering.** Think back, this is not just a momentary glance to the past but a charge to reenter those feelings, those thoughts of the days when love for God guided every action, determined every footstep. It is like going somewhere and then realizing that you were going in the wrong direction. Discovering your error, you realized that there was no shortcut or alternate route. The only answer was to retrace your steps back to the beginning and start again from there. That is what Jesus told the Ephesians to do.

2. **True repentance always involves a humble acknowledgement that although wrong is admitted and perhaps mourned, there is no right to expect a restoration to a place or position held before.** A false repentance is marked by an attitude that says, "I asked for forgiveness. Now, you forget everything and give me what I want." A true repentance says, "I have done wrong and though you have forgiven me, I realize there are consequences for my actions that cannot be erased in a moment." The criminal may have repented, sought and found God's forgiveness, but the jailor is under no obligation to open his cell and set him free.

---

⁹*Sam Storms, To the One Who Conquers: 50 Daily Meditations on the Seven Letters of Revelation 2-3. 50*

Theater of Ephesus, used for games, plays, public speaking, and persecution of Christians.

3. **True repentance accepts discipline and accountability.** Words of commitment are proven by actions and humbly submitting to those who will help the offender be vigilant against the tendency to slip back.

4. **When remembering brings the truth of how far you have fallen away, don't just feel remorse.** Turn around. While remembering should take some time, repentance needs to be a decisive act in the present moment. Not one more step along this dead end path. Not one more breath without love. Not one more day wasted.

5. **Do the first things again.** Once more become as a child, teachable and ready to listen. Damn the dignity if it causes a moment's hesitation. It is like Christ is saying, "You are so concerned about the straying of

others but it is you, dear Ephesians, who have strayed away from Me. I want you back. Retrace your steps until those steps lead you back to Me. Don't stop until you find your way again."

There are dire consequences for failure at this point. Jesus warned that He would remove their lamp stand. The term for remove indicates that it will be done with "deliberation and judicial calmness; there would be no sudden uprooting as in anger, but a movement which would end in the loss of the place that the Church had been called to fill; unless there came a change for the better, the first of seven lamps of Asia must disappear."[10] Failing to repent and return when love has been lost is to allow the flame to flicker out, its light gone to leave the world darker than before.

But you have this in your favor: You hate the practices of the Nicolaitans, which I also hate (Revelation 2:5).

There is a change in tone again. Reclaiming love should not come at the expense of seeking truth. They are not mutually exclusive.

Of concern here is a group known as the Nicolaitans. The word is made up of two Greek words: *nike,* which means, "to conquer" and *laos,* which means "the people." The name spells out their ambition. They meant to conquer the people with their teaching.

The Nicolaitans are mentioned nowhere else in the New Testament outside the book of Revelation. Not much is known about them. They seemed to have flourished for a short time and then either imploded or were absorbed by other heresies. There is some thought that they were an early form of the Gnostic heresy. Irenaeus wrote about them in *Against Heresies,* saying that they denied the Trinity, the dual nature of Christ and the transcendence of God. They believed that God the Creator was an inferior being from God, the Father. Further, they believed that Christ was simply a good

---

[10]*Beacon Bible Commentary,* 496

man, that at His baptism the divine "Son" possessed His body, abandoning Him at the crucifixion.[11]

According to Win Groseclose, United Evangelical Protestant Church pastor and teacher, Nicolaitans seemed to have advocated that meat offered to idols could be "exorcised" of any evil and therefore eaten at pagan festivals. They surrendered to the immorality of the city, believing that after a week of any indiscretion they could be fully restored to the fellowship of the church with no follow up consequence. Some think that they justified their actions by saying that the practices of the unbelievers were empty and therefore could not harm the Christian since the pagan gods didn't exist. Some even felt that they were deepened spiritually by their depraved acts. The danger of such teachings in the church was of deepest concern, especially to new believers who came out of an immoral background.

Jesus commended the Ephesians for hating their practices as He said He did. The biblical understanding of hate means to be separated and to reject. It is not an emotion of disgust but of distinguishing between what is right and wrong. The Nicolaitans were not to be hated but their works were. Restoration was needed for them from the error of their teaching and life just as it was for the Ephesians for their loss of love.

Whoever has ears, let them hear what the Spirit says to the churches. To the one who is victorious, I will give the right to eat from the tree of life, which is in the paradise of God (Revelation 2:7).

The closing to this message ends with a promise that resonated with Ephesian believers.

The Temple of Artemis contained a tree shrine, a place of "salvation" for the worshipper. The temple, it will be remembered, was a sanctuary that protected those inside from any enemy. But the temple ended up sheltering unrepentant criminals who brought corruption to the city. It promised something it could not deliver.

---

[11] *Win Groseclose, Letters to the Seven Churches.* 11

Christ sets that perversion of God's intention against His purpose for the believers. He promises them "the tree of life, which is in the paradise of God." Interestingly, the word for "cross" never appears in the book of Revelation. However, the Greek term for tree has various meanings. The most frequent usage was for a plant but it was also often used to indicate an instrument of punishment. The term "tree" was used by the early Christians to refer to the cross as seen in Acts 5:30 and 16:24. In this setting it is likely that Christ, in naming the tree of life was in fact, saying that it is His cross that is the means of life. And while the Temple of Artemis promised refuge, it in fact became a place of great evil. But the paradise of God is not like that. It is a true place of refuge where sin cannot enter, where the worshipper and lover of God is absolutely safe.

Ephesus might boast the Temple of Artemis but the believer in Christ lays claim to the tree of life in the paradise of God.

Discussion Questions

1. What challenges did the Temple of Artemis present to the Christian community in Ephesus?

2. There are varying views as to who the angels are that Christ addresses. Why is this important or not important?

3. When it is proper to compromise and when should we hold firm?

4. Think of some public figures who have suffered disgrace because of some sexual indiscretion. Who showed true repentance? How did they do it?

5. Why can a Christian not just claim grace and do whatever he/she wants even if it is defined as sin in Scripture?

IN THE BALANCE

Personal Reflection

1. Caesar worship required an annual confession of Caesar as lord and then the person was allowed to return to his/her religion. Why would a Christian risk dying by refusing to conduct a five-minute ceremony? Is there any compromise in your life that seems trivial but causes you to name something else as lord?

2. When are the times that you have compromised and wished you hadn't? What caused you to give in? What were the costs because you did so?

3. Is there anything in your life from which you need to repent? What steps do you need to take? How will you know if you have genuinely repented?

4. When you think of the tree of life, what comes to mind?

Revelation 2:8-11
To the Church in Smyrna

8 "To the angel of the church in Smyrna write:

These are the words of him who is the First and the Last, who died and came to life again. 9 I know your afflictions and your poverty—yet you are rich! I know about the slander of those who say they are Jews and are not, but are a synagogue of Satan. 10 Do not be afraid of what you are about to suffer. I tell you, the devil will put some of you in prison to test you, and you will suffer persecution for ten days. Be faithful, even to the point of death, and I will give you life as your victor's crown.

11 Whoever has ears, let them hear what the Spirit says to the churches. The one who is victorious will not be hurt at all by the second death."

SMYRNA:
Pressed But Not Distressed

— Revelation 2:8-11

Whether it was in Great Britain, the United States, Canada, Switzerland, France or elsewhere, the early years found The Salvation Army under constant and severe persecution. Its outdoor meetings were attacked by mobs that threw stones, rotten fruit and vegetables, pushed down and beat them. Rather than protecting them, police arrested Salvationists as disturbers of the peace because their presence irritated people. Scorned by most established churches as well as being the brunt of jokes and caricatured in the press, The Salvation Army was a magnet for every kind of abuse. Because it sought to reach the very poor, many feared its work would lead to unrest among the masses. Others found its uniforms and military style of "church" to be amusing at the very least, something to ridicule and physically assault by rougher hands. Many took offense at its brand of confrontational Christianity that demanded a response to the question, "Are you saved?" The founder of The Salvation Army, General William Booth, was maligned and pilloried in the press, suspected of exploiting his followers by skimming great sums of money from its coffers for his personal use. Despite audits and close inspections of its work by government and private individuals and despite their inability to substantiate any of the scandalous claims, some of the slander stuck to the fledgling organization anyway. The Salvation Army existed in a constant state of poverty, buffeted by attacks on every side even as it expanded around the world.

One morning there was a particularly ruthless attack in the

Smyrna, a faithful ally of Rome, built the first temple of the Emperor Tiberius.

editorial section of the *London Times*. Bramwell Booth, Chief of the Staff and eldest son of the aging General Booth, complained bitterly to his father about the ill treatment the Army was receiving. Wisely, General Booth replied, "Fifty years hence it will matter very little indeed how these people treated us. It will matter a great deal how we dealt with the work of God."

The people of Smyrna understood the kind of attack that issued that kind of response.

The Glory of Asia

The ancient peoples associated Smyrna with the reality of death for good reason. Its very name reminded them of myrrh, a medicinal spice that was also used in preparing a body for burial. Myrrh literally means "bitter" and that description in many ways fit it, too. Smyrna's name seemed to trumpet the certainty of suffering.

Its history testified to the death image as well. Founded in the

IN THE BALANCE

11th century B.C., for centuries the city enjoyed great prosperity and power. But when the Lydian Empire began to expand, Smyrna was the first point of attack. Initially, it rebuffed the attacks, forcing the invaders to retreat and adding more territory to its own kingdom as a bonus. But its pride and laziness became its later undoing. When again the Lydians under Croesus attacked around 580 B.C., the city fell. In their rage, the Lydians leveled Smyrna until all that was left of the once great city was a series of small villages. For all intents and purposes, Smyrna was dead, its past greatness forgotten despite being the birthplace of Homer, the great Greek writer of classics such at *The Odyssey* and *The Iliad*.

It remained insignificant until Alexander the Great came 400 years later. After viewing the ruins of the ancient city, Alexander slept under Smyrna's old acropolis. That night he dreamed he was to build a new city on this site. He immediately set to work by moving the city closer to a natural spring, then gracing it with wide and straight streets, a luxury in the ancient world. The city boasted a new marketplace, gymnasium, stadium and theater that seated 20,000 people. Its harbor was of great strategic importance because it could be totally enclosed in times of war to protect a fleet from attack. New temples were erected on Mount Pagos that rose above Smyrna, dominating its skyline. The temples ringing Mount Pagos resembled a crown around the mountain as the marble shone in the sun. It was a spectacular city that had risen from the ruins, and soon was dubbed "The Glory of Asia." An earthquake later destroyed the city in 177 A.D. In grief over its destruction, the Emperor Marcus Aurelius suspended taxation on the city for 10 years to allow it to rebuild.

When the Roman Empire was only beginning to form, the city of Smyrna was one of the first to ally itself to the new ascending power. They fought with the Romans against the Seleucids who ruled one of the Greek remnants of Alexander the Great's former empire in Asia. When the Romans were fighting the Mithridites, the Smyrneans sacrificed their own clothing to send to the freezing forces of Rome. Its alliance with Rome was so strong and pronounced that in 195 B.C. a temple was erected to *Dea Roma*, where the city of Rome was personified as a goddess. It was no surprise that despite several cities vying for the honor of erecting the first temple to Emperor Tiberius, Smyrna was selected. The Roman historian, Livy, called Smyrna *pro singular fide;* "singularly faithful" while Cicero, the great Roman orator and politician said of Smyrna that it was Rome's "most faithful and ancient ally."[12]

To the angel of the church in Smyrna write: These are the words of Him who is the First and the Last, who died and came to life again (Revelation 2:8).

Christ identified Himself to the church in Smyrna in a similar way as He did in the first chapter of Revelation. "I am the Alpha and the Omega," said the Lord God, "who is, and who was, and who is to come, the Almighty" (Revelation 1:8) and "I am the First and the Last" (Revelation 1:18).

The Smyrnean Christians were suffering terribly, a minority people who were dogged with persecution and plagued with poverty. Their resolute determination to hang on was admirable but they needed reassurance. Christ gave that to them by reminding them that they belonged to the One who had absolute power, who defined not only the present moment but all of eternity as the first and the last, the never beginning beginning and the never ending ending. No event, no period of time compared with that. He was in it with them but also above the stream of time that He Himself ruled. History did not happen to Him. Rather, He initiated and directed it. As the first, He is the source. As the last, He is the destiny of all that is living. When all this is gone, Christ reminds them, I still am.

He further identified Himself as the one "who died and came to life again." The Smyrneans would remember their own history of a once prospering and alive city, destroyed and in the grave for 400 years. But it was now alive again, more glorious than before. The city's rebirth was an illustration of Christ's glorious resurrection.

But it went further than that. Each year at the festival for

---

[12]*Ulery, 39*

Dionysius, the death and rising of the god was enacted and celebrated, not with solemn gratitude but with drunkenness and depravity. That resurrection was a mockery as it led to shameful acts of sin and abuse. But Christ's resurrection was an inescapable fact leading to holy lives of honor.

When John heard this from Christ as he wrote the message to the Smyrneans, how he must have marveled again as he thought about the resurrection of Christ. What is treated by present day Christians as an almost routine fact, to the early Church was a subject of unending amazement. No sermon could be preached without reference to it. The epistles constantly come back to this startling and thrilling moment when everything changed. John would think back to his moment of realization as he stooped at the entrance to the tomb, stared in and believed. The resurrection of Christ had not only changed that Sunday morning, but every moment that would take place after that. Every saying, every miracle, every action of Christ's during His earthly ministry had layers of meaning that before the resurrection could not have been imagined. Writing about it later, John said, "If every one of them were written down, I suppose that even the whole world would not have room for the books that would be written" (John 21:25). So, dear Smyrnean believers, recall that the marshaled forces of evil did not defeat the One you worship. He rose triumphantly over them! He was the one "who died and came to life again."

I know your afflictions and your poverty—yet you are rich! I know about the slander of those who say they are Jews and are not, but are a synagogue of Satan (Revelation 2:9).

The Nature of Suffering

As Jesus turned His remarks directly to the church at Smyrna, He recognized the condition that was the unavoidable fact of their lives. They were suffering to a degree that was suffocating. The Greek word for "afflictions" is thlipsis, which means to be pressed or squeezed. It is comparable to someone trapped between two rocks while being compressed between them more and more. The original word also described a threshing roller used to grind wheat or crush grapes.

It is important to distinguish between the suffering that comes to everyone in the course of living life and that which is specific to the Christian walk. Both believers and unbelievers suffer from ill health, poverty, discrimination, disaster, disability, heartbreak and are victims of war. The Christian is not placed in some impervious bubble that screens germs, deflects bullets or filters out cruel remarks, nor can he expect that his pantry will magically restock itself after every meal, or that the bends in the road will straighten before him. As Jesus said, "(The Father) causes His sun to rise on the evil and the good, and sends rain on the righteous and the unrighteous" (Matthew 5:45). There is a democracy that exists in the fallen world that spares no one and singles out no one for more or less suffering based on their pedigree, as punishment for their life in the womb or any supposed previous life that is birthed in their imagination. Both godly and ungodly parents have children who are born with congenital issues or who suffer from injury or disease, whose every moment is marked by pain. As Jesus showed in His ministry, they are not singled out for suffering because they have sinned and are being punished. To be sure, because of circumstances, some enjoy favored status by simply being born in the right place or in the right family. Others enjoy a healthful and relatively pain-free life while some go from one tragedy to another, one diagnosis followed by another one more serious. But all people will know suffering. And if it is not known in the present moment, it will make itself known at some point very soon.

While the believer can take this kind of pain to the Lord and find His comfort and help, the Christian needs to be very careful not to find virtue in suffering that would be his regardless of what he believed. My genetic condition is not a badge of righteousness. It is because I am born in the human race, a child of Adam with a body that at once serves me well and then at another time is at war with itself.

The difference between the Christian and the non-Christian with

At one time a cistern supplied Smyrna with water. Later Alexander the Great moved the city closer to a natural spring.

this kind of pain is that while the believer cannot avoid suffering, he can show the world how to suffer. If that suffering leads eventually to physical death, his life can be a testimony of how the God who helped him to live can now help him to die triumphantly. Simone Weil has remarked, "Each time we have some pain to go through, we can say to ourselves quite truly that it is the universe, the order and beauty of the world and the obedience of creation to God that are entering our body. After that, how can we fail to bless with tenderest gratitude the Love that sends us this gift?"[13]

The Smyrnean believers suffered the same aches, pains, diseases and difficulties common to all the people living in Smyrna in that day. But this is not the suffering that Christ is referring to in this passage. The tribulation they knew was specific to their stand for Christ. If they just had not declared their allegiance to the Savior, life would have been simpler, less painful.

Nor were the Smyrneans told by Christ to hang on a little lon-

---

[13] *Arthur Wells, Inspiring Quotations Contemporary and Classic. 193*

ger, that help was on the way. The suffering that was in the present would be followed by more suffering and, as we know from history, the persecution grew fiercer, more widespread until each Christian home could see in itself a potential martyr. As Sam Storms says, "Instead of asking, 'Why do Christians suffer persecution?' we ought to inquire, 'Why do Christians not suffer persecution?'"[14]

The very human tendency is that when pain comes we want it to stop. While we may understand that suffering must happen, we tend to understand it in a generic sense until it clings unwanted to us. We expect blessing but are surprised by suffering. Our Bibles are underlined with the uplifting verses that promise good things, but seldom do we seek to dwell on those passages that tell us that pain is the mark of the believer, that naming Christ as Savior means to own the cross He sets before us. We would think it odd if someone asked for prayers that he might suffer because we are so used to prayers being solicited for suffering to stop. But it is in those tender and lonely moments of pain, especially pain felt because of our stand for Christ, that we perceive what it means to truly live for Christ. Paul cried out, " I want to know Christ—yes, to know the power of His resurrection and participation in His sufferings, becoming like Him in His death" (Philippians 3:10). So here the Smyrnean believers shared space with Christ on Mount Calvary, not as observers in a crowd but hanging on their crosses next to His.

The Pain of Poverty

Not the least of the trials was the pain of poverty. This was not the uncomfortable paycheck-to-paycheck variety but utter destitution bordering on vagrancy. Why would this be in such a prosperous community as Smyrna?

Although there were wealthy converts to Christianity from the beginning, it found its most ready audience among the poor and the slaves. This was already a time when famine did not just create shortages but people starved to death en masse. When natural

---

[14]*Storms. 68*

disaster struck, homes were destroyed with no agency coming alongside to help the family recover. If on a journey through the desert drinking water was lost or thieves stole the food, it meant that, short of a compassionate passerby, a slow, painful death was certain. When an invading army swept through the countryside, they wasted no time making friends of the inhabitants but instead stole all, kidnapped, enslaved, raped and murdered, scorching the earth with the flames of burning villages.

Polycarp, a Christian bishop who was burned alive in Smyrna.

That most of the Christians were poor or slaves meant they were already vulnerable, already life was precarious. But when they were also Christians, a merchant could refuse to sell to them, an employer could elect to hire someone who shared his religious beliefs. Countless Christians around the world know what it is to have jobs, education, and benefits denied them because they have not aligned themselves with the official religion of that country. It is an old but effective tactic of the enemy of souls. Such conditions were well known to the believers in Smyrna.

Increasingly, the Christians suffered from the attacks of mobs that destroyed their shops, burned their homes and stole their possessions with official sanction. With no protection from a hostile and unsympathetic government, they were left to watch their livelihoods and possessions go up in flames or be carried off by criminals who had no fear of prosecution.

After the fall of Jerusalem, a massive number of Christians entered Smyrna and were subjected to slander from the Jewish community.

There were also Christians who purposely sought to live on less, to the point of destitution. Whether it was money or gifts received from family and friends or earned income, they saw an opportunity to give it away to the glory of God. Liberal gifts were given out of a heart grateful to God that did not count any cost too high in response. Gifts were given out of compassion to help alleviate the desperate conditions of other Christians who suffered. Some, knowing the hold that possessions had on them, chose to cast them aside so that they could have an unhindered life of service and devotion to Christ. An example of this comes to us from the fifth century in Arenius, a man who was determined to live a holy life. He abandoned the comforts of Egyptian society to follow an austere lifestyle in the desert. Yet whenever he visited the great city of Alexandria, he spent time wandering through its bazaars. Asked why, he explained that his heart rejoiced at the sight of all the things he didn't need.

Slander

What caused further difficulty for the believers was the slander that was leveled against them. Much of it arose from misunderstanding or deliberate misrepresentation of what Christians believed and practiced. The Greek word for slander is more correctly translated "blaspheming," indicating the ferocity of the words and intent. Lord Alfred Tennyson called it, "the meanest spawn of Hell."[15]

British author Malcolm White summarizes six recurring slanders against the early believers:

1. Because they celebrated Communion and spoke of the "body and blood" of the Lord Jesus they were accused of being cannibals.

2. Because they called their common meal agape or "love feast" they were accused of holding orgies and being immoral.

3. They were accused of splitting families because some believed and some did not. (This one was solidly founded on fact.)

4. They were accused of atheism because they did not have idols to worship.

5. They were accused of being politically disloyal because they would not swear allegiance to Caesar.

6. They were accused of being "gloom and doom" merchants because they preached the end of the world at the return of Jesus.[16]

What was probably most distressing about the slander is that primarily it originated in the Jewish community. So corrupt was this group that Jesus called them "the synagogue of Satan." The

---

[15]*Oxford Dictionary of Quotations*, 538
[16]Malcolm White, *You've Got Mail.* 66

Jewish people in Smyrna were long established and highly influential. While they may not have had much in common with the pagan worship of the Greeks, Romans and other Gentile religions, they allied themselves with them against the Christians. What was an annoyance early on as Christians began to show up in Smyrna following Pentecost, seemed to spin out of control when there was a massive influx of Jewish Christians following the destruction of Jerusalem by Titus in 70 AD. Whether their motivation was protection of Judaism or a mean spirit aimed at easy prey, the slander scorched the believers.

What makes slander so hard to handle? Slander is hurtful because so very often it is anonymous. It can come as a question, "Do you know what people are saying?" or as a frontal attack that is disorienting in its intensity. But what "they" say can sometimes be answered with no guarantee that truth will neutralize lies. John Stott observes, "We should not be too greatly concerned by the opinions of unbelievers, but rather cultivate the mind of Christ. Only He can see straight; all others are to some degree cross-eyed and squint."[17]

Do not be afraid of what you are about to suffer. I tell you, the devil will put some of you in prison to test you, and you will suffer persecution for ten days. Be faithful, even to the point of death, and I will give you the crown of life (Revelation 2:10).

Sensing their dread, Jesus told the Smyrneans, "Do not be afraid." The same thing was said to John in Revelation 1:17 but the phrase, "Do not be afraid," appears a total of 365 times in the Old and New Testaments, one for every day in the year. The command is not to stuff our feelings but to feel relief that God is in control of the situation and the moment when we feel overwhelmed. More times will come. But the Lord is in those moments and like the manna, provision of strength or an answer or the grace to endure will be with us at the moment of trial.

---

[17]*Stott, 43*

Imprisonment

Imprisonment is mentioned specifically. The prisons that existed in the ancient world were nothing like modern correctional facilities, some of which are little more than country clubs for "white crime" offenses. Sir William Ramsay explains, "Imprisonment was not recognized by the law as a punishment for crime in the Greek or Roman procedure. The State would not burden itself with the custody of criminals, except as a preliminary stage of their trial, or in the interval between trial and execution. Fine, exile and death constituted the normal range of penalties; and in many cases, where a crime would in modern times be punished by imprisonment, it was visited with death in Roman law."[18]

From anywhere in the city Mount Pagos shone with its ring of temples. But also up on that mount there was the prison. The Smyrnean believers could constantly see the place that might be their final destination. In sharing with them that they would be imprisoned, Jesus was effectively telling them they were under a death sentence. It might be immediate or as a prelude to deportation to Rome or some other arena for the games. How poignant then were His words, "Do not be afraid."

Curiously, Jesus gave a cryptic message, saying that the persecution would last 10 days. There is almost universal agreement among scholars that this was not a reference to a literal 10-day period, but symbolic. But symbolic of what?

One theory states that it represents a near literal count as the amount of time between arrest, trial and execution. Some see the number 10 as symbolic of completion, of totality. Some say it means an infinite amount; others think it means a limited time. Still others see it as representing something that will last for a lifetime. It is impossible to know for certain now but very likely the Smyrneans and the early Christians understood it. In this context it sounds like a word to encourage, not an indefinite sentence.

---

[18]*Ramsay, 292*

Be Faithful

Smyrna understood the virtue of faithfulness. The city had early allied itself to Rome and through the years had proven itself a true friend, regardless of the political and military realities in the region. Rome could count on Smyrna even in the bleakest hour. The people of Smyrna were proud of this quality in themselves. Christ now called the Smyrneans, known for their loyalty, to be loyal to Him through whatever came next.

Being faithful in Smyrna meant to live their lives in an environment so hostile that a simple walk in the neighborhood posed a risk. It meant that when Christians went out in the streets to share the good news of Christ, they couldn't know for sure if they would return in good shape or nursing injury. It meant that even as they could see the dark clouds of persecution gathering above them, they would not retreat to a safer place. As they labored at the jobs no one else wanted for wages that could not sustain them, they believed they were kept by something greater. For far too many, it would mean holding true as the lions and other wild beasts were unleashed or as they were tortured for the amusement of the idle. Being faithful was to know that no pain could equal the glory promised to the ones who were true.

Crown of Life

The crown of life is a metaphor for eternal life but that symbolism would have had even more impact in Smyrna.

The "crown of Smyrna," the source of civic pride, was that ring of temples on Mount Pagos that made the city famous. But these buildings eventually crumbled. The crown of life was not subject to such decay.

Royalty received their crown to signify their high office, their authority to reign. Earthly sovereigns sought that moment of coronation when a crown was gently rested on their heads. But Jesus told the suffering Smyrneans that at His appearing that just as He received His crown, He would also give them theirs.

The people of Smyrna were well familiar with the celebration of

IN THE BALANCE

Theater of the god Dionysius, who was honored annually at a drunken ceremony of death, burial and resurrection.

Dionysius, whose worship was centered there. The annual festival included the mock death, burial and resurrection of the god. The priests were given crowns that were composed of olive branches or similar plants. But Christ's resurrection was no bit of stage acting, but the truth of the ages. The crown of life would not wilt like those of Dionysius but remain flourishing in eternity.

When my wife and I were serving in The Salvation Army in St. Petersburg, Florida, one of our social programs included Sallie House, an emergency shelter for abused and neglected children. Preteen children were placed there immediately upon removal from their homes to either be relocated with extended family members or to go into the foster care system. While at Sallie House, the children attended Sunday school at The Salvation Army.

One day Stephen, a twelve year old, showed up at Sunday school and shared how he had once been one of those children at Sallie

House. He told of the day he came to Sunday school and as part of the activities, there was a treasure hunt that involved the children looking for chocolate filled "gold" coins. Stephen shared that he found the most that day and as a result, he was crowned the king of Sunday school. At a time when his young life was falling apart, he reigned for five minutes as king with a cardboard crown and a makeshift robe. The joy of being crowned had never left him, even if it was only for a few minutes.

An ancient coin minted in Smyrna.

For the Christians in Smyrna whose world was threatening and who in a moment might be swept away in the next wave of persecution, Jesus promised that they would be given an imperishable crown of life. The thought of that joy bred an irrepressible hope.

He who has an ear, let him hear what the Spirit says to the churches. He who overcomes will not be hurt at all by the second death (Revelation 2:11).

Amid the ominous content of His message to Smyrna, Jesus consoled them with a promise that related to death. As fearful as death might be in this life, the persecuted and faithful Christians need not fear an even greater threat: the second death.

The Jews were very familiar with the concept of the second death. It was to be eternally and totally separated from God. The anguish of such a state is seen in Jesus' parable of the Rich Man and Lazarus (Luke 16:19-31). The Jews thought only those who were Hebrew by birth or had converted to Judaism and accepted all of its ritual (including circumcision) could enter Heaven. Christ was speaking to a largely Gentile audience of believers or Jewish believers who were excommunicated from the synagogue because of their allegiance to Christ. Jesus assured them that despite the bitter denunciations of the Jews who opposed them, they need not fear the doom of the second death.

So even death was not to be feared. The life that was theirs because of their relationship with Christ secured them against that.

Polycarp

The attitude of this church was never more clearly seen than a few short years later by Polycarp, their bishop.

On Saturday, February 23 in 155 A.D., the city of Smyrna was packed with crowds who had come to watch the bloody and vicious public games in the arena. Not happy with the carnage before them and thirsting for more, a cry went up, "Away with the atheists! Let Polycarp be searched for." (Christians were called atheists because they did not accept the Roman gods.) Although he could have escaped and had ample warning, Polycarp had a vision the night before in which he saw the pillow under his head on fire. He awakened to tell his disciples, "I must be burnt alive."

When a slave under torture gave away his whereabouts, the guards came to arrest him. As they entered the house, Polycarp instructed those present to feed them a meal while he asked for one last hour to pray. The police captain hated his duty and on the way into the city, said, "What harm is it to say, 'Caesar is lord' and to offer sacrifice and so be saved?" But Polycarp refused to even consider that option.

When he entered the arena, the proconsul gave him the choice of cursing the name of Christ and making sacrifice to Caesar or face death. In one of history's most stirring replies in the face of certain doom, Polycarp boldly declared, "Eighty and six years have I served Him and He has done me no wrong. How can I blaspheme my King who saved me?" When the proconsul threatened to burn him alive, Polycarp answered, "You threaten me with the fire that burns for a while and is quickly quenched, for you do not know the fire which awaits the wicked in the judgment to come. Come, do what you will."

At that the crowds rushed forward with the wood to heap around him. When they sought to tie him to the post, he said, "Leave me as I am for He who gives me power to endure the fire will grant me to remain in the flames unmoved." So they left him there, set the fire and Polycarp died. Those who were standing around said that the aroma smelled like baking bread.

Be faithful, though in poverty. Be faithful, though beaten down. Be faithful, because the Lord whose riches surpass all measure will lift you up and give you the crown of life.

Discussion Questions

1. The city of Smyrna remained a faithful ally of Rome throughout the empire's history. How did that example of faithfulness of the citizens play out in the lives of the Smyrnean believers?

2. The author says that general suffering is not the same as suffering specifically for Christ. How then should we view common suffering and God's willingness to comfort us?

3. In what way are Christians slandered today? What should their reaction be to it?

4. Jesus told the Smyrnean Christians, "Do not be afraid." How does a person remain calm in the face of suffering?

5. Discuss how the story of Polycarp's death affects you.

IN THE BALANCE

Personal Reflection

1. Jesus identified Himself to the Smyrnean believers as the "Alpha and Omega." How does that identification assure you when you are going through difficult times?

2. Can you think of a time when you specifically suffered for Christ? If so, what were your feelings at the time? Did your suffering glorify the Lord?

3. Some early Christians deliberately chose poverty in order to share with other poor believers. Have you ever sacrificed financially to the point of your own detriment for other believers who are suffering more? If so, why did you do it? If not, what would stop you?

4. Tell how you suffered slander because of your stand for Christ.

5. Jesus promised the believers who endured a crown of life. Share the moment you imagine when Christ presents you with your crown.

Revelation 2:12-17
To the Church in Pergamum

12 "To the angel of the church in Pergamum write:

These are the words of him who has the sharp, double-edged sword. 13 I know where you live—where Satan has his throne. Yet you remain true to my name. You did not renounce your faith in me, not even in the days of Antipas, my faithful witness, who was put to death in your city—where Satan lives.

14 Nevertheless, I have a few things against you: There are some among you who hold to the teaching of Balaam, who taught Balak to entice the Israelites to sin so that they ate food sacrificed to idols and committed sexual immorality. 15 Likewise, you also have those who hold to the teaching of the Nicolaitans. 16 Repent therefore! Otherwise, I will soon come to you and will fight against them with the sword of my mouth.

17 Whoever has ears, let them hear what the Spirit says to the churches. To the one who is victorious, I will give some of the hidden manna. I will also give that person a white stone with a new name written on it, known only to the one who receives it."

PERGAMUM:
Unwise to Compromise

— Revelation 2:12-17

riving through the streets of Port-au-Prince soon after the devastating Haiti earthquake of January 12, 2010, I was amazed to often see one building still standing while the one next to it had literally crumbled into dust. While there were many reasons why buildings collapsed, the most outstanding one went back to how they were constructed in the first place. In order to save money, steel reinforcement was not used or if it was, employed sparingly or improperly made. When reinforcing steel rods were used they tended to be smooth on the outside instead of having the recommended deformities in the re-bar that allow concrete to better adhere to them. In addition, an inferior grade of sand was used in mixing the concrete. While the buildings looked identical after construction, when the quake came most of the structures with proper concrete and steel reinforcement remained standing. The others, in testimony to the compromises made in construction, tumbled to the ground. Hundreds of thousands of Haitians either lost their lives, their limbs or were badly injured as a result. Still tens of thousands more lost their homes. What seemed like a harmless way to shave expenses and pocket the difference produced not places to live but places to die.

Capital of Asia

At the time of the New Testament, Pergamum was the proud capital of the province of Asia. But because it was not on any of the major trade routes it was very poorly located for commerce. That would lead to its decline over time. But when John wrote, the city was one of the largest in the world, with close to 200,000 people. The exceptional statuary that had no equal in that part of the world beautified it.

Pergamum was divided into an upper and lower city. The citadel sat on top of a steep hill that rose a thousand feet (300 meters). Thick walls studded with watchtowers gave it further protection. Although it was a formidable fortress, there was no natural water supply, a deadly danger during a siege. Massive cisterns were created to catch the rainwater that in turn led to reservoirs. Supplementing this system was an aqueduct that crossed the Kozer Plain, bringing water to the lower city. Connecting the upper and lower cities was a road that led down to its famous medical center.

Founded originally in the early third century B.C., Pergamum was never conquered by the Romans. Instead, in 133 B.C. the dying King Attalus III, with no heirs to assume the throne after him, turned the city over to Rome in his will. The early alliance with Rome allowed it to enjoy not only victory in battle but great favor as well.

The Library at Pergamum

With its collection of over 200,000 volumes, Pergamum's library was second only to the great library in Alexandria, Egypt. There was a great rivalry between the two cities, not only to have the greatest collections but in an incident that had wide ranging consequences, personnel as well.

In a move to gain a clear advantage, Pergamum tried to hire away the esteemed head librarian of Alexandria, Aristophanes. When the king in Alexandria heard it, he put the librarian in jail and then, to punish Pergamum, cut off its supply of papyrus. Made from the reeds that grew by the Nile, papyrus was the only material used for writing at the time. Faced with not only losing Aristophanes as their librarian, Pergamum also found the vital supply of papyrus gone. The future of their library itself was in jeopardy.

The people of Pergamum were known for their ingenuity. It

Pergamum was one of the largest cities in the world, with a population of about 200,000.

wasn't long before they learned to make an exceptionally fine paper from animal skins that not only replaced papyrus but also was longer lasting and of much higher quality. The paper derives its name from the city: parchment.

Later, when the library of Alexandria was destroyed by fire, Antony looted the library in Pergamum, giving its collection to Cleopatra as a gift. But when Octavian, later Caesar Augustus, won out in his civil war over Antony, he replaced the stolen volumes, reestablishing the greatness of the library in Pergamum. This act was never forgotten in Pergamum.

The Medical Center
Occupying a place of honor and prominence in the lower part of the city was the Aesculapian, the medical center and temple to the god Aesculapius. The symbol for Aesculapius is a rod entwined by snakes, still in use by the medical profession today. Of great concern

PERGAMUM: Unwise to Compromise

to the Christian believers was not only that Aesculapius was another false god but also that he was known as Asklepios Sōter, "Aesculapius the Savior."

Bishop Terence Kelshaw of the Anglican Church in North America, describes the center and some of the procedures a person had to follow to gain his healing.

> … The remains of the temple of Aesculapius, which in its day was 120 feet high, the walls richly painted with scenes depicting the god of healing at work. At the center of the room, a sole piece of furniture today, stands a short, round, stone pillar four feet high, carved on the side with two intertwined snakes, the sign of the god of healing. The top of the stone was slightly concave and a small fire burned there continuously, for this was the altar to the god Aesculapius, where visitors were met by a priest and obliged to buy a measure of incense to be deposited upon the flames as a votive offering of trust in Aesculapius. A slave then led the patient through intimidating huge brass doors into a large park skirted about with colonnaded walks on all sides. At the center of the park was a villa which housed the sacred pool, with priests in attendance, where the patient was taken and invited to step down into ankle-deep water while the priest ascertained the symptoms of the illness before determining the level of votive offering, or payment, required for the healing.
>
> … the patient bartered with the priest toward a reasonable price to appease Aesculapius and secure the healing. If it was enough, then water would flood into the pool but, if not, only a trickle would appear. Since effective healing was possible (but not guaranteed) only if the water rose to waist level, the first sum discussed was never enough! Bargaining would continue until the price reached what was considered by the priest to be satisfactory for Aesculapius to send enough water into the pool.
>
> Once positive-thinking attitude was established the patient was given a sacred mud bath and then transferred to the herbal bath, where a strong drug vapor was inhaled. When the patient was sufficiently sleepy from the drug vapor he was taken for a long walk through the "whispering corridor," so named for the soft whispering voices of the court of Aesculapius which could be heard wafting from the ceiling as they sang encouraging ditties of healing. Shafts of light seemed to shine down on the patient even from where the court was singing. Excavation has revealed that on the roof of

---

[19]Kelshaw, 57, 58

the corridor were openings that had small chimneys that focused the light of the bright sun into the corridor. Groups of priests stood around and sang gentle songs into the chimney, creating an echoing, mysterious sound.

By the time the patient reached the far end of the whispering corridor he was heavily drowsy and high on spirituality and drugs.

Once the effects wore off patients made their way back to the villa, where more positive-thinking psychotherapy could be administered, which might be followed by further sacred mud treatment or quiet convalescence at the villa.

Available to the convalescent were gardens in which to walk, a theater, a library, conversation in the philosophical hall, or one could simply relax on the covered terraces and drink in the view of wonderful Mother nature.[19]

The center specialized in diseases of the digestive track using a treatment regimen of exercise, music, drama, literature and rest. It also included a theater that sat 3500, allowing patients to perform plays for each other. At night they were taken into the temple that was filled with tame snakes where in the darkness the snakes glided by them. Since snakes were the symbol of Aesculapius, patients were encouraged to believe that the touch of the snakes was the same as touching the god himself.

Religious Life and the Imperial Cult

Pergamum boasted the largest statue of Zeus in the ancient world displayed on an enormous platform that stood 800 feet (240 meters) above the city, resembling a throne. It was commonly believed that Zeus was born in Pergamum. Adding to the normal drama of Zeus' worship, the priests were able to manipulate the platform to cause billowing smoke and the statue to move so that it appeared to be alive.

The cult to the Egyptian god Sarapis thrived in Pergamum as well. Honored as the god of fertility as well as the sun god, some Gnostics would later claim it was this god that was the creator of the material world.

As troublesome as were the worship of these gods and others in

---

[19]*Kelshaw, 57, 58*

the Greek and Roman religion, none would cause as much trouble for the Christians as the Imperial Cult. Pergamum was especially zealous in promoting and enforcing the idolatrous worship.

Likely out of gratitude to Augustus for restoring their precious collection to the library from Alexandria, in 29 B.C. the citizens of Pergamum were granted permission to erect a temple to their benefactor. It was the first time a temple had been erected to a living emperor. A worshipper was to kneel before the statue of Augustus while burning incense as he was saying, "Caesar is lord." This was an annual requirement for all people in the Roman Empire, and a certificate was issued to show compliance. After that, the person was free to go back and worship his other gods or none at all. Both Jews and Christians refused to participate in Caesar worship. While there was some persecution of the Jews as a result, the full blow of resentment crashed down on the Christians. It was here in

The Aesculapian, a medical center and temple to the god Aesculapius, specializing in diseases of the digestive track.

Pergamum that the first Christians were taken to court for their disobedience. And it was here that they were first condemned to death for refusing to comply.

To the angel of the church in Pergamum write: These are the words of Him who has the sharp, double-edged sword. I know where you live— where Satan has his throne. Yet you remain true to my name. You did not renounce your faith in me, not even in the days of Antipas, my faithful witness, who was put to death in your city—where Satan lives (Revelation 2:12-13).

Christ identified Himself as having a two edged sword, a weapon that was a uniquely Roman innovation in warfare. This type of sword was reserved for high officials in the Roman government as a symbol of their authority. To have a two edged sword was to have what was called jus gaddi, the right of the sword. Those so empowered could pronounce the sentence of death on an individual. The proconsul in Pergamum was the only one in the province of Asia who held this right.

For the believer, it is remembered that the Bible refers to itself as a two edged sword. "For the word of God is living and active. Sharper than any double-edged sword, it penetrates even to dividing soul and spirit, joints and marrow; it judges the thoughts and attitudes of the heart" (Hebrews 4:12). While the Roman proconsul might have the power to condemn the Christians to death for their non-compliance to the Imperial Cult, the Savior proclaims that His power is in His Word that can discern the hidden thoughts and intent of people.

The church in Pergamum was commended for standing true. The term "not denied" is written in the Greek aorist tense, meaning that it refers to a specific point in time when an action was taken. The moment of testing came, fierce and strong, but the church did not wither from the blows. It stood firm.

Apparently fresh in the minds of the church in Pergamum, an otherwise unknown believer named Antipas gave his life for the

Faith. His name means, "against all odds" or "against all opposition." Legend says that he was roasted to death in a brass bull as a human sacrifice in the rites for one of the gods. In his dying, Antipas gave witness to his faith. The true meaning of the word "martyr" is witness. For the Christians to witness was to risk death. The word morphed to encompass that reality. The truth that had dawned on the believers of Pergamum was that Antipas' fate was not an isolated case but that he represented the first example of the way things were going to be.

Given the surroundings where they served, they stood in sharp contrast to those around them. In speaking of that, Jesus not only said that this is the place of Satan's throne but where he lived. The great platform of Zeus' temple was a constant reminder of how alien they were in their own hometown.

The hostile surroundings, however, were not enough for the Christians to sound retreat. Nowhere are Christians urged to relocate to friendlier climes. The witness must be in the place where the believer is found. Battles are not won by deserters but by those who stay to fight. Transformation of a home, a town, a culture will not happen by a believer taking up his cross and fleeing but by taking up the cross and following. That may mean bearing it in places so wicked that Satan reigns unchecked. The throne was the symbol of that authority but the influence of Satan permeated every part of life in Pergamum. This was the battleground. Here is where the Christians of Pergamum must make their stand.

> *Nevertheless, I have a few things against you: You have people there who hold to the teaching of Balaam, who taught Balak to entice the Israelites to sin by eating food sacrificed to idols and by committing sexual immorality. Likewise you also have those who hold to the teaching of the Nicolaitans.* (Revelation 2:14,15).

While they stood firm against persecution, the church in Pergamum allowed the enemy to sneak in the back door. Perhaps they were feeling hopelessly outnumbered where they lived and anyone who shared at least some of their beliefs seemed like an ally. Some might have argued that inviting in those who had drifted into heresy was a good thing. That way the church could have a purifying effect upon them. Sadly it seldom works that way.

Samuel Logan Brengle, the great holiness preacher of The Salvation Army, wrote, "A stick that is about straight is still crooked." The infection spreads in a healthy body, contamination works its way through pure water. That is what happened when the Nicolaitans and the Balaamites were welcomed without censure into the body of believers.

Recall that the Nicolaitans were also a problem in Ephesus. The difference here is that they were more than allowed an entrance but were permitted to take up positions in the church. Their teaching was put alongside the pure word of the gospel. This resulted in the Scriptures warped to support their doctrine.

While it may seem that there are two different groups being talked about, they were likely synonyms for each other. Those called Balaamites were guilty of the sin of Balaam. The long and rather strange tale of Balaam is found in Numbers 22-24. To summarize the story briefly, as the Israelites were moving into the Promised Land there was growing apprehension in the nations that were already there. There was good reason for that. A number of powerful kingdoms had already been defeated while there was no abatement in the progress the Hebrews were making. With military strategy and fortified cities equally ineffective, Balak of the Moabites called on a prophet of the Hebrew God YHWH, to bring a curse on them. Since they were obviously conquering because of God, it seemed that only God could stop them.

Balak took Balaam to a spot in the mountains where he could see a portion of the Israelites in camp. Balak explained what he wanted and offered a huge reward if Balaam was successful. To his surprise and utter dismay, Balaam answered, "Even if Balak gave me his palace filled with silver and gold, I could not do anything great or small to go beyond the command of the Lord my God" (Numbers 22:18). Despite this, Balak urged him to curse the Israelites. Balaam instead blessed the people of Israel, sending Balak into a rage. The scene was repeated twice more and each time Balaam blessed the Israelites rather than cursing them. If the story ended there, Balaam might be one of the great heroes of the Old Testament. But the lure of riches was not easily put aside.

The wealth promised by Balak was enough to make Balaam work out another strategy for the Moabites. If God would not curse the Hebrews, they could be made ineffective by moral erosion. So Balaam counseled Balak to send Moabite women into the Israelite camp to charm and seduce the enemy (Numbers 25). This they did and with disastrous results, leading the Israelites not only into sexual sin but worship of the Moabite gods. While Balaam's strategy worked, he never enjoyed the fruit of his scheming. When the Israelites sought their revenge against the Moabites, Balaam was killed (Joshua 13:22).

The Balaamites and Nicolaitans in Pergamum were guilty of the same sin of perverting the people of God by appealing to sensual appetites and leading them away from Him. It was already difficult enough to avoid entanglements. Kent Ulery notes, "The meat from the sacrifices on the altar of Zeus, along with the meat sacrificed on the altars of Pergamum, was the same meat served at banquets, the same meat for sale at the agora (marketplace), the same meat available in restaurants, and the same meat brought to potlucks."[20] Trying to avoid these occasions for compromise was a minefield for the Pergamum believers. The Nicolaitans and Balaamites simply asked, "Why bother? What's the harm? Meat is meat." Their words were meant to entice or to use the meaning of the Greek, to literally, "cast a stumbling block" before someone to lead them to sin. The Balaamites and Nicolaitans would further reason that if it were acceptable to eat this meat in private, why not in public? The festivals to the gods were cultural events, times of fellowship, they would reason. Just eat the meat and enjoy yourself. And in sitting down to eat, the temptation was to enter into other activities more

---

[20]Ulery, 54

The temple of Zeus was displayed on an enormous platform that stood 800 feet (240 meters) above the city and resembled a throne.

grossly sinful, tougher to overcome.

Aspringius of Beja, ancient commentator on Revelation, notes that, " ... 'Balaam,' which is interpreted 'without people' or 'without property.' For Balaam is a type of adversary who does not gather a people for salvation, nor does he rejoice in the number of the multitude to be saved. Rather, as long as he destroys all and remains without a people and without any property, then he rejoices."[21]

That is why the church of Pergamum could not afford to compromise, to sit at the table with the enemy to enlarge on the points of agreement while minimizing the differences. There are associations, which by their very nature are destructive. While the Christian must maintain a love and yearning for the salvation of the lost, it cannot be done at the expense of truth or the undoing of his own experience. Some people must be loved from afar until they show

---

[21]*Ancient Christian Commentary, Vol. X, 30*

that they are ready to repent or at least own that their way is faulty. Beyond that, there are times that our inherent weakness in some area makes us easy prey for those who would rather bring us down to their level than rise to the standard of holy living.

The example found in the story of King Saul's jealousy and seething anger toward David is a sad one. For ten years he pursued David across the nation of Israel with the sole intention of killing David, who was not only his son-in-law but remained fiercely loyal to the king. Twice David spared King Saul's life when he had it in his power to take it. Witness that after Saul admitted the unrighteousness of his murderous intention, David nonetheless could never be near Saul again. (1 Samuel 26:17-25). The association was too destructive for David. He must love him from a distance. The story ends, "So David went on his way, and Saul returned home." Though David may have loved King Saul, he knew that being near him was a death wish. The Pergamum church had to realize that since the Nicolaitans and the Balaamites had not responded positively to the loving concern for the believers but instead had poisoned the church, it was time to separate from them.

Repent therefore! Otherwise, I will soon come to you and will fight against them with the sword of my mouth (Revelation 2:16).

The only path was repentance. It was not because there was any virtue in rejecting people but for the health of the body of Christ. Sir William Ramsay has observed, "An easygoing Christianity could never have survived; it could not have conquered and trained the world; only the convinced, resolute, almost bigoted adherence to the most uncompromising interpretation of its own principles could have given the Christians courage and self-reliance that were needed. For them to hesitate or doubt was to be lost."[22]

There can be no revival without heartfelt repentance. It is difficult to admit that we have been guilty of wrong, that in the

---

[22]*Ramsay, 322*

liberality of our love we have permitted too much, that we have retreated when we should have stood firm. But the way forward is first to go backwards. To fail to do so is to perhaps be popular with the world but to grieve the Holy Spirit, and as this passage says, to face the anger of an offended Savior.

The threat of Christ to fight against the evildoers is not words of peaceful coexistence but the threat of utter extermination to those who would resist Him. The words are harsh and unyielding. This is the language of purging, of burning out the impurities. The Lord leaves the option before the church in Pergamum. Either they will deal with the evil ones among them or Christ will. And gentleness is not on the agenda.

He who has an ear, let him hear what the Spirit says to the churches. To him who overcomes, I will give some of the hidden manna. I will also give him a white stone with a new name written on it, known only to him who receives it (Revelation 2:17).

The overcomer is promised that he will receive the hidden manna. The story of God's provision of manna for the Israelites while they were in the wilderness continued to resonate centuries later. When Moses finished the Ark of the Covenant, we are told, "Moses said to Aaron, 'Take a jar and put an omer of manna in it. Then place it before the Lord to be kept for the generations to come'" (Exodus 16:33). The eventual fate of the Ark of the Covenant has been left to legend, but one of the strongest traditions is that Jeremiah hid the Ark with its contents somewhere in the environs of Jerusalem or the nearby mountains. In this way, the manna was hidden along with the Ark. An account of this legend can be found in the apocryphal book of 2 Maccabees 2:4-7 and again in the apocryphal book of 2 Baruch. The Jews believed that the hidden manna would reappear when the Messiah established His kingdom. The promised manna for those who were faithful stood in sharp contrast to the meat offered to idols that compromising Christians were then eating. The idea is that the faithful will feast on the true bread of the kingdom.

A white stone is also promised. The exact meaning of this is not fully known but there are several thoughts, all with merit for the believer.

1. Although there is no evidence of the practice occurring in Asia, it would have been known to the people of Pergamum that gladiators who had survived five years of fighting in the arenas, were given their freedom signified by a white stone with the letters "SP" on it, standing for the word spectatus, meaning "tried and proved." The faithful Christian received a white stone that was akin to the words of the parable, "Well done, good and faithful servant" (Matthew 25:23).

2. Another idea comes from the religions of that day that offered an amulet with a secret message inscribed that was supposed to protect the wearer from harm. Christ is offering to the believer His own secret inscription that would keep him in the evil day.

3. White stones were used in calculations. So the Christian who did not waver was counted faithful.

4. White stones were used to signify great days in the life of a person. The believer's great day of salvation as well as the victorious entry into the Lord's presence in death or when He returns was that white stone.

5. Rather than a paper ticket that admitted people to events such as exists in the present time, white stones were given to allow the bearer into events or to receive benefits from the government. Our white stone signifies our entry into God's presence with all the benefits attending that.

6. The Church Fathers saw it as signifying adoption as a child of God. We are co-heirs with Christ through our adoption into the family of God.

7. When called upon to judge, each member of the jury was given a white stone to signify a vote of "not guilty" and a black stone to signify "guilty." The believer receiving a white stone has acquitted him of all wrongdoing, proclaimed "not guilty" by virtue of his justification by faith.

8. When a victorious general returned from war, he was given a white stone to guarantee that his living henceforward would be at the expense of the empire. So the believer entering eternity knows that all is well, that he shall never suffer need again.

The stone comes with a new name written on it. Again, the meaning of this is not entirely clear but scholars theorize it can mean one of several things or a combination of them.

1. Sam Storms offers, "God will rename each of us in accordance with the transformation of our nature into the likeness of His Son, to reflect the new and altogether unique identity each has received by grace ..."[23] Our new name will be a perfect reflection of our redeemed character and will summarize the story of our life in Christ.

2. The word for "new" is not the one that means recent in time but rather "fresh." This carries the idea that there is an eternal and joyful freshness that comes with our eternal life in Christ demonstrated by our new name.

3. The ancient people believed that there was power in the very name of the gods. Recall that the Jews were so careful with God's name that in the Scriptures they substituted the word "Lord" where His proper name appears. So holy did they consider God's name that some scribes would use

---

[23]*Storms, 101*

a new quill to write it and then never use it again. To know the name of a god was to be able to call on him or her, to have a claim for protection or intervention. The name given by the Lord, in this interpretation, is His own name allowing the believer special access.

Caesar Augustus restored the records stolen by Mark Antony to the Pergamum library after his defeat of Antony.

4. The new name can also reflect the new character that comes with being born again. This is a new life. In some places in Asia today, it is very common that when a person turns to Christ as Savior, while retaining their birth name, they begin to also be called by a Christian name to signify their new life. Often these are biblical names, showing that the believer has claimed his new life and by taking the new name, declaring that God now has ownership of them.

In a clever portrayal of Christian faith and warfare, C.S. Lewis in Screwtape Letters records a series of letters from an older, experienced demon named Screwtape to his younger, inexperienced nephew Wormwood. Screwtape rarely counsels his young charge to make a frontal assault on the Christian he is trying to attack but rather advises that he use more subversive tactics so that doubts arise, ardor cools, and the believer is distracted. It is in the easing of the Christian's defenses that he is most likely compromised, his witness neutralized. The tactic described by Lewis in his fictional book had been proved in the real world of Pergamum.

IN THE BALANCE

Discussion Questions

1. Aesculapius was known as a "savior." What modern saviors seek to be a substitute for Christ?

2. The early church struggled with what to do with Christians who bowed to the image of Caesar and called him lord. Some believed they should be freely forgiven but others believed they should go through a set discipline to be restored. Who do you think was right? Why?

3. Imagine that a leader in your church was arrested for his witness, tried and then martyred for his faith. What effect would that have among your fellow believers?

4. How does the story of Balaam serve as a warning to believers?

5. When is it better to love from a distance rather than risk harm to ourselves?

Personal Reflection

1. Have you ever "knelt down" to something in your life and declared it to be lord instead of Christ? What would tempt you to do so again?

2. The people in Pergamum had to take their stand in a place Jesus called the "throne of Satan." Where do you need to take your stand?

3. Can you think of a time when you thought you could positively influence someone for the Lord but instead you found you were negatively affected instead? Why did that happen?

4. The author notes that, "in the liberality of our love we have permitted too much, that we have retreated when we should have stood firm." When was this true for you? What actions did you take to correct it?

5. Imagine the day that Christ hands you your white stone. What will He give as a reason for you to have it?

IN THE BALANCE

Revelation 2:18-29
To the Church in Thyatira

18 "To the angel of the church in Thyatira write:

These are the words of the Son of God, whose eyes are like blazing fire and whose feet are like burnished bronze. 19 I know your deeds, your love and faith, your service and perseverance, and that you are now doing more than you did at first.

20 Nevertheless, I have this against you: You tolerate that woman Jezebel, who calls herself a prophet. By her teaching she misleads my servants into sexual immorality and the eating of food sacrificed to idols. 21 I have given her time to repent of her immorality, but she is unwilling. 22 So I will cast her on a bed of suffering, and I will make those who commit adultery with her suffer intensely, unless they repent of her ways. 23 I will strike her children dead. Then all the churches will know that I am he who searches hearts and minds, and I will repay each of you according to your deeds.

24 Now I say to the rest of you in Thyatira, to you who do not hold to her teaching and have not learned Satan's so-called deep secrets, 'I will not impose any other burden on you, 25 except to hold on to what you have until I come.'

26 To the one who is victorious and does my will to the end, I will give authority over the nations— 27 that one 'will rule them with an iron scepter and will dash them to pieces like pottery'[a]—just as I have received authority from my Father. 28 I will also give that one the morning star. 29 Whoever has ears, let them hear what the Spirit says to the churches."

THYATIRA:
The Enemy Within

— Revelation 2:18-29

Few who were living and aware on September 11, 2001 will forget the day or the scenes that were replayed repeatedly on television. First one jet crashed into the World Trade Center in New York City. Then as that tragedy was being shown viewers watched live as another jet crashed into the second tower. It was learned that still another airliner had plowed into the Pentagon and that another attempt was aborted with a plane down in Pennsylvania. Later it was revealed that the last airliner was destined for the Capitol building in Washington, DC. The world joined the United States in swift action. Security was tightened at airports and other modes of mass transit. Borders were made more secure. Laws were enacted to control the funding of terrorist organizations. Those traveling into and out of countries at risk were monitored much more closely. Communications were interrupted or tapped. Although numerous large-scale follow up attempts were made within the United States to follow up on the September 11 attacks, none succeeded.

But the danger remained. Bali and Jakarta suffered bomb attacks in an attempt to strike out at Australian citizens. Soon in the United Kingdom and then elsewhere new waves of terrorist attacks were conducted by citizens within the country. Arab nations battled virtual civil wars that many times began as unrest against unjust governments but soon were infiltrated by terrorist organizations. Africa continued to experience wide ranging flare-ups across the continent, most of which were kept aflame by training and financial

THYATIRA: The Enemy Within

Ancient ruins of Thyatira, whose main function was to slow down an invading army for the more important city of Pergamum.

support from terrorist organizations.

Homegrown terrorism added another battlefront. No longer was the enemy "out there" but among us, able to travel without restriction, walk about freely, striking at any time without warning. Interviewing neighbors after these attacks yielded a similar series of remarks. "He seemed like a nice enough guy." "I would never have expected it of them." "I'm shocked. To think that someone like that lived right next door."

For Thyatira, the enemy no longer was banging down the door. She was hosting dinners, inviting the whole church to join her as she dined in shameless splendor and open defiance.

Expendable Defense

Unlike the other cities studied thus far, Thyatira never was a city of great importance. It is however, strategically located about 30 miles (50 kilometers) outside of Pergamum. Its main function historically was to slow down an invading army long enough for the more important city of Pergamum to prepare for battle. Unfortunately, it was not well suited as a defensive stronghold. There was no hill upon which to build substantial fortifications, no natural lines in the landscape that could be used to strengthen their position. Its destiny in battle was to always be a pawn to be sacrificed, doomed to be overrun as the invading armies eventually pushed their way through.

Although it did not fare well as a garrison town, it was wonderfully located for manufacturing and commerce. Half the ancient world's trade travelled through Thyatira. It lay in a rich and fertile valley that produced abundant crops. There were rich mineral deposits that generated a lively industry for metalworkers, especially bronze for which Thyatira had world renown. Because it benefited from a booming business, residents enjoyed wealth and prosperity.

Thyatira's most favored deity was Apollo, the sun god. But Thyatira's name indicates that this was not always the case. The name of the town is made up of two words that mean "castle of Thea," the latter name indicating it was originally dedicated to a now unknown female deity.

Trade Guilds

What distinguished Thyatira was the strong and influential presence of a series of trade guilds. Trade guilds bound together craftsmen in similar fields to allow them fellowship, collaboration, quality control, management of competition and the kind of influence that numbers could give for issues of mutual interest. So powerful were the guilds that no one could afford to refuse joining one if it existed for his particular craft. Declining to link with a guild would put him in a highly vulnerable position to enduring intimidation by the guild members, to limiting the purchase of raw materials or the sale and transport of finished goods. It was an ancient equivalent to a closed shop that allows trade unions to restrict all the hiring in a certain business to members of the union.

It was not the benefits of trade guilds that caused problems for the Christians. It was the social life that attended membership. All guilds honored the gods, but usually there was one god in particular that served as a patron. Guild meetings always began with a sacrifice to the god followed by a meal. It was the practice that the meat offered in the sacrifice would be cooked and eaten by the guild members. Christian guild members would first have to endure the rites of worship to the patron god, the sacrifice to his or her honor and then be expected to eat the meat that a few moments ago had been the offering. It will be remembered that when Gentiles were allowed full membership into the church, only two restrictions were placed upon them. They must abstain from sexual immorality and they must not eat meat offered to idols (Acts 15:29).

The difficulties did not end there. As the night wore on there was heavy drinking often followed by public and private acts of coarse joking, free flowing profanity and gross immorality. The Christian was assaulted at every turn in the guild meetings. He was faced with one of two very difficult choices. If he remained a guild member, his convictions were under hours of long attack in the meetings and constant calls to compromise in the workplace. If he did not attend the meetings or left the guild, he could be committing professional and financial suicide.

What happened at the guilds was not uncommon across the whole Roman Empire. The conduct in guild meetings reflected what happened in almost every phase of life. Outside of the Jewish religion, moral purity was virtually unknown in the Roman Empire, especially when it incorporated the lax morality of Greek society following the conquest of Greece. It was said at this time that a man had a wife to bear his children, a mistress to take to social occasions and a lover for sexual satisfaction. What would now be considered child sexual abuse was allowed without question and even promoted as a way to educate youth about sex. One of the shocking discoveries when Pompeii was excavated was the proliferation of murals displaying what would be characterized now as grossly pornographic scenes. Portrayals of sexual activity between children and adults are not uncommon.

The consistent teaching from Christians was that none of this was permitted nor could it be tolerated within the church or its members. When people complained that to live a pure life and separate from these behaviors meant financial ruin, the answer was that they must stand strong. Tertullian wrote, "Must you live? There are no musts where faith is concerned."

The church in Thyatira found itself in this most challenging situation of trying to make a living on the one hand and the countercultural demands of Christianity on the other.

To the angel of the church in Thyatira write: These are the words of the Son of God, whose eyes are like blazing fire and whose feet are like burnished bronze. I know your deeds, your love and faith, your service and perseverance, and that you are now doing more than you did at first (Revelation 2:18-19).

For the only time in Revelation, Jesus identified Himself as the Son of God. The description that follows is not only one of strength and brilliance but is a direct answer to the local veneration of Apollo, god of the sun. Apollo was often portrayed with gleaming eyes. But Jesus claims that for Himself.

That was not the only reason His claim as the Son of God was important. At this time in the early history of the church, people were still trying to work through who Jesus was. They knew of the historical Jesus who walked among them, was crucified and resurrected. But exactly what His nature was remained controversial, causing a great deal of turmoil. The apostles insisted that Jesus was a once-and-for-all person that was both fully divine and fully human. Others struggled with that. Theories abounded with almost every conceivable combination of divine and human natures. Some thought that He was a good man that God singled out for His Holy

Spirit to descend upon but who removed Himself from Jesus at the crucifixion. Others believed that He was half God, half man but that the two natures continued to be separate, side-by-side without comingling. The Gnostics taught that He was a combination of both divine and human but more human than divine, one among many emanations from the true, good god. To them He was a link in a chain, not the unique Son of God. An early form of Gnosticism was already causing problems in the church, some of which will be discussed later in this section. Answers to this heresy already marked the New Testament as seen in the letter to the Colossians as well as being sprinkled through the other letters of Paul, John, Peter and the unknown writer of Hebrews.

In Jesus identifying Himself as the Son of God and in bright glory at that, He was asserting His unique place as the full expression of God to humanity. Two features are specifically mentioned. His flaming eyes spoke of His penetrating gaze that could read what was in the hearts of people. Fire, a frequent symbol of judgment in the Old Testament, spoke of God's anger toward those who would stand in rebellion against Him. The blazing eyes are searching eyes, the flames illuminating the darkness of hearts in opposition to Him.

Feet like burnished bronze stand for judgment as well and His walking with authority in all of creation. This is military language because bronze was the favorite metal for weapons of war. Thyatira was known for its superior bronze weapons, fired in furnaces of brightest flame. Christ the conqueror stood on feet that made the best earthly weapons pale in comparison.

As a judge, Christ knows. He proves this in what He had to say to the Thyatirans. First, He commends what He has found.

He spoke of their service, which literally means, "to wait on tables." Theirs was a genuine expression of love in the humble spirit of Christ who washed the disciples' feet. Their perseverance was not seen to be standing up under trial like a person trying to walk through hurricane winds but rather a positive and steadfast endurance through everyday life. It was showing up every day, though each day was most certainly filled with opposition, insults and

Apollo, the sun god, and the most popular god in Thyatira.

Christ Weighs the Hearts of 7 Churches

THYATIRA: The Enemy Within

Thyatira had powerful trade guilds for craftsmen, and membership was largely unavoidable.

hardship. This was a witness that would not be driven away by sneers, but one that proved itself in the moments of every day.

But as John Stott has noted, "The church of Thyatira displayed love and faith, service and endurance, but holiness was not included among those qualities."[24] It was busy doing and perhaps by the sheer amount of activity, it saw itself as righteous. But works and holiness cannot balance each other on some cosmic scale. Neither can compensate for the other. They are more like two wheels on a common axle than they are negotiable quantities interchangeable with each other.

Nevertheless, I have this against you: You tolerate that woman Jezebel, who calls herself a prophet. By her teaching she misleads my servants into sexual immorality and the eating of food sacrificed to idols. I have given her time to repent of her immorality, but she is unwilling. So I will cast her on a bed of suffering, and I will make those who commit adultery with her suffer intensely, unless they repent of her ways. I will strike her children dead. Then all the churches will know that I am He who searches hearts and minds, and I will repay each of you according to your deeds (Revelation 2:20-23).

These verses contain one of the sharpest denunciations of a specific individual in the New Testament. Although the believers in Thyatira were mostly Gentiles, the reputation of Jezebel may have already crossed into popular culture so that her name was synonymous with evil, much like Hitler's name in our day even though people may not know much about the Second World War. It is

---

[24]Stott, 68

doubtful that the woman was actually named Jezebel, the infamous queen married to Israel's King Ahab who together led the most wicked reign in Jewish history. Although her actual name may be masked from us now, she was easily recognizable to the Thyatirans and likely was present when this letter was read publicly. New Testament scholar Colin J. Hemer suggests, "It may have been a shock to hear this popular teacher equated with Jezebel. The church may well have denounced and shunned the grosser forms of syncretic paganism in the city while harboring teaching which ... imperiled those whom it led into the very same evils."[25]

There is speculation that she was the wife of Thyatira's bishop. That alone would have given her considerable influence. Another less likely possibility is that she was a local and well-known soothsayer named Sambthe, who mixed black arts with Jewish and Christian teaching, not unlike what is done with the Voodoo religion of the present day. Sambthe had a shrine just outside of Thyatira.

The lady Jesus called Jezebel may not have been either one of these. Although she is called a prophetess, it is likely an honor that was self-given as opposed to what was recognized in Christian circles as the gift of the Holy Spirit.

As in the twenty first century, first century Christians had to constantly be on guard against the tendency of syncretism: the combining of elements of other religions into Christianity. Although a new convert's heart was immediately changed through the act of conversion, the head took a little longer to come around. Without the sound teaching of Scripture and doctrine, it is easy to drift into error when answering a convert's questions or challenging a believer's acts. This is especially the case where an individual is the sole believer in a family that has little or no concept of Christianity or the Bible.

What makes this all the more difficult is that the teaching of other religions is not all bad. Forms of the Golden Rule can be found in most organized religions as well as admonitions to tell the truth,

---

live morally and take care of the family. There is also wisdom to be found in their writings, some of which parallels Christian truth. But a similarity of a number of teachings does not mean that other religions are on an equal footing with Christianity.

Jezebel was not so much opposed to what Christians believed as she was interested in expanding it to include other teachings as well. She was advocating a less restrictive range of behaviors so that Christians could fully participate in the trade guilds and life in Thyatira. According to her, attending the heathen festivals was just becoming part of civic life. It was okay to eat the meat offered to idols if business prospered as a result. Bowing to a god didn't matter since the god was false anyway. It was only a gesture. "Loosen up," Jezebel would purr, "Life's too short to get hung up on a bunch of rules."

To bolster her claim, as indicated by claiming to be a prophetess, she no doubt claimed special revelation from God. Like any false prophet she asserted that her revelation was more important than what had been written centuries ago or even what Christ had taught a few years back. That such an idea would have gained footing in Thyatira is evidenced by the fact that the church there later slipped into the heresy of Montanism, which held that the Holy Spirit was continuing to reveal truth beyond that which was found in the Bible. The difficulty always arising from such a view is the claim of the new revelation either being superior to the Scriptures or having some mystical insight never before known. While Christians believe that the Holy Spirit helps interpret the Word of God in their hearts, He does not replace the Bible with some special insight nor will the Holy Spirit ever lead believers in a teaching that contradicts what is clearly spelled out in the Bible.

No doubt she urged a tolerance of other religions, or tolerance for behaviors and lifestyles contrary to the teaching of Scripture. She was likely very persuasive and able to maneuver verbally with more grace and speed than those who tried to stand against her. In the setting of Thyatira such a view of Christianity would have been welcome because it would have allowed people to claim a righteousness that was not married to righteous living.

The sad thing is that few in the church even attempted to speak out against her. From the Scripture portion before us, somehow Jezebel was addressed, was given the opportunity to repent but in her pride and self-righteousness, she lived in defiant rebellion.

The spirit of Jezebel did not die with this woman in Thyatira. There have always been calls for the Church to abandon the high moral ground, to join the mainstream whether that is in sexual morality, political issues, or corporate and individual greed. Whole denominations have lost their authority to speak on issues of faith because of the so-called openness to lifestyles and teachings that contradict the Bible or have been seduced by the lure of wealth and materialism. That was the place where Thyatira found itself. Because it had lowered the standard instead of being salt and light it had become irrelevant in the religious life of the city where it was to bear witness.

Judgment for Jezebel
If the people of the church would not act, Christ assured them that He would. Jesus warned that He was going to cast her into a bed of suffering. That can mean several things, all of which would fit. First, since she was committed to allowing for adulterous activity, the place of her immoral acts would become the place of her moral execution. Secondly, it can be an expression for being restricted to a deathbed, never recovering health or strength. Thirdly, the Greek word for a banqueting couch, *kline,* is used here, indicating she may be struck down while enjoying one of her compromising feasts. Those who followed her, her children, will also suffer God's wrath. The literal translation is that He will "kill them to death." It means to strike them dead with no chance for survival.

Jesus reminded them that He is the one who searches hearts and minds. The original language actually uses the terms for kidneys and heart. In ancient thinking, the kidneys were thought to be the seat of the emotions while the heart was where thoughts were centered. The NIV changes this to our more modern use of the heart for our emotions and the mind for our thought. The point of it is that the Lord is saying there is not a thought or a feeling that He will not examine. This is a warning to the one who rebels against Him but great consolation to the one who sincerely loves and follows the Lord. To the one who has dishonored Christ in his decisions, the examination will be painful and humiliating. To the one who has sincerely loved his Lord, the examination will show that although the actions were not always perfect, the love and intention were pure toward God. While we cannot always be flawless in our actions due to human frailty, we can be blameless before God in our intent.

Now I say to the rest of you in Thyatira, to you who do not hold to her teaching and have not learned Satan's so-called deep secrets, 'I will not impose any other burden on you, except to hold on to what you have until I come.' (Revelation 2:24-25).

Not everyone had bought into the teaching of Jezebel. They purposely turned away from her, perhaps boycotting her teaching or openly standing in opposition to her. With what might be a reference to Gnosticism, Jesus spoke about "Satan's so-called deep secrets." Those teachings would have included the ethical practices that Jezebel urged as outlined above. The term "deep things" in Greek is *ta bathea,* a motto used by an early Gnostic sect that claimed it had insight into deeper secrets about God. Supposedly, by opening themselves up to a broader view of Christianity they would be rewarded with a deeper, more mysterious and exclusive spiritual experience. Occult practices would have been included to enhance this "enlightened" approach.

The Lord assured the small group of beleaguered believers that there would be an end to their vexation. No more difficulty or pressure would be put upon them. Their responsibility was to remain faithful. William Barclay wisely counsels, "There are two essential things in Christianity. One is the victory, and the other is a long fidelity. The Christian life does not consist in one victory over sin; it consists in a lifelong fidelity that defies every assault of sin. The Christian life is not a battle; it is a campaign."[26]

IN THE BALANCE

Thyatira lay in a rich, fertile valley that produced abundant crops.

To the one who is victorious and does my will to the end, I will give authority over the nations— that one 'will rule them with an iron scepter and will dash them to pieces like pottery'—just as I have received authority from my Father. I will also give that one the morning star (Revelation 2:26-28).

The closing of this letter would have deeply resonated with the Thyatirans.

First, they were to be given authority over the nations. What welcome news that must have been to a city that had served as a buffer in wartime between two opposing forces, whose survival or safety was not a concern to either an invading army or the country to which it belonged. Their city was nearly defenseless, positioned strategically in the path of the aggressor but reckoned

---

[26] *Barclay, 65*

to be expendable by the larger city of Pergamum. It had never been able to hold off anyone, never able to rpel the forces arrayed against it. The citizens of Thyatira knew that when an enemy army was in view, they could not stop it. Soon they would be overrun and underfoot again.

But here Christ promised them that they, the downtrodden Thyatirans, would have authority over the nations! Could they believe it? The authority would not come from Pergamum or from Rome or any other earthly power. The authority over the nations would come from Christ Himself. Reading the book of Revelation later they would find an angel of Heaven proclaim, "The kingdom of the world has become the kingdom of our Lord and of His Christ, and He will reign for ever and ever" (Revelation 11:15). The nations would be His. No matter how they had armed themselves or proclaimed their own might, the nations would meekly surrender to the Almighty God. He would once again remind them that the territory they ruled was never theirs to begin with. Christ's ownership gave the promised power. And these downtrodden Thyatirans would stand in league with the victorious Christ. Christ proclaimed that His rule would be absolute. An iron scepter, the symbol of irresistible power, would be in His hand.

The reference to broken pottery would be very familiar throughout the ancient world. When potters discovered that their final work was defective, they shattered it to pieces. The pottery craftsmen of Thyatira dumped their broken pots in a common place outside the city known to all. The picture of total brokenness and irreparable destruction showed the futility of resistance to the conquering Christ.

Finally, Christ promised the overcomer he would receive the morning star. The morning star is the planet Venus, which had been an emblem of authority from the time of the Babylonians. It was the claim of the Caesars that they descended from the goddess Venus, giving them the right to rule. The reference in this setting is beautifully explained by Tyconius: "It is appropriate that we understand the morning star to represent both Christ and the first resurrection, because His appearance scatters the darkness of error and the worldly shadows of the night are put to flight by the approaching resurrection. For as this star brings an end to night, so also does it mark the beginning of the day."[27]

Discussion Questions

1. How should Christians behave when practices at their workplace or school are in direct opposition to their Christian faith?

2. How can even righteous acts detract from holy living?

3. What marks a Jezebel in the church?

4. Many believe that all religions lead to Heaven. What does the Bible say about this belief?

5. William Barclay describes the Christian life as "not a battle but a campaign." What does that mean?

Personal Reflection

1. The Thyatirans had to often choose between working and their Christian faith. Have you faced such a choice? What did you do?

2. Read what is said about syncretism. Where have you seen this played out?

3. The Thyatirans failed to speak out against the false teaching of Jezebel. If you were to meet her, what would you say to her?

4. Although we are not always perfect in our actions God sees the intent of our hearts. Think of when you have meant well but it turned out poorly. How does this view of the Lord cause you to think about it now?

5. Christ promised the Thyatirans that those who were faithful would be rulers over the nations. Describe what that means to you.

IN THE BALANCE

Revelation 3:1-8
To the Church in Sardis

1 "To the angel[a] of the church in Sardis write:

These are the words of him who holds the seven spirits[b] of God and the seven stars. I know your deeds; you have a reputation of being alive, but you are dead. 2 Wake up! Strengthen what remains and is about to die, for I have found your deeds unfinished in the sight of my God. 3 Remember, therefore, what you have received and heard; hold it fast, and repent. But if you do not wake up, I will come like a thief, and you will not know at what time I will come to you.

4 Yet you have a few people in Sardis who have not soiled their clothes. They will walk with me, dressed in white, for they are worthy. 5 The one who is victorious will, like them, be dressed in white. I will never blot out the name of that person from the book of life, but will acknowledge that name before my Father and his angels. 6 Whoever has ears, let them hear what the Spirit says to the churches.

7 "To the angel of the church in Philadelphia write:

These are the words of him who is holy and true, who holds the key of David. What he opens no one can shut, and what he shuts no one can open. 8 I know your deeds. See, I have placed before you an open door that no one can shut. I know that you have little strength, yet you have kept my word and have not denied my name."

SARDIS:
Church of the Living Dead

— Revelation 3:1-8

I n 1974, some Chinese farmers digging a water well stumbled onto one of the greatest archaeological finds of all time. Below the surface was a magnificent terracotta army complete with weapons, horses and chariots, an estimated 8,000 foot soldiers, court officials, acrobats and strong men. For centuries they had silently guarded the tomb of Emperor Qin Shi Huangdi. The construction of his tomb began shortly after he took the throne at age 13. The details of the figures are incredible—for example, each soldier has a different face. They were painted to make them look even more realistic. In the end, even the best artists could not make them look perfectly lifelike. Even if an artist could, looking alive is not the same as being alive.

In Sardis a church existed but it was actually filled with dead people walking. It appeared alive but on closer inspection, the life was gone.

Golden Past

The kingdom of Lydia began in the twelfth century B.C. and at its peak eventually covered roughly the western half of modern Turkey. Never overly ambitious in its quest for territorial gains, it was a wealthy kingdom more concerned with protecting what was its own. The capital was Sardis, an impressive city whose most prominent feature was what was considered an impregnable fortress. Perched high atop sheer cliffs, its substantial walls added to the height and image of invincibility. With a vast internal support for food storage and water supply for the city, an invading army could only be frustrated with any attempts to directly assault or lay siege to take the citadel. As long as Sardis stood, the kingdom of Lydia would not fall.

What made Sardis so attractive was not only its strategic placement as a port city and the intersection of five major roads, but its incredible wealth. The River Pactolus that flowed through the city was laden with gold dust. In myth, Midas was able to get rid of his golden touch by washing in the springs of Pactolus. The springs then had the golden touch, turning the sand into gold. Gold was also discovered and mined in the surrounding mountains. If that were not enough, the metallurgists of Sardis discovered a process to separate gold from silver. This revolutionized how gold and silver were used. Now objects and jewelry could be certified as solid gold. It also made a marked difference in currency since it was now known that a gold coin was in fact, pure gold. With this technology in hand, Smyna became the first kingdom to mint coins. To provide a proper weight for measuring gold, Croesus used the seed of the carob tree. Carob evolved into the word "carat," the standard to measure weight in precious gems and metals to the present day.

Sardis reached its peak in wealth and influence during the 14-year reign of King Croesus. For centuries afterwards, a saying to indicate a person's great wealth was to say he was "as rich as Croesus."

Another rich resource for Sardis was its famous wool. A process had been discovered there for dying it. The sheep in the surrounding countryside were particularly valued for the quality of their wool. The ability to dye this high quality wool brought great prominence to Sardis.

Fortress of Folly
But the wealth of its city and its formidable fortress eventually worked against Sardis. The Greek historian Herodotus tells how Cyrus, the Persian, in 549 B.C. invaded Lydia. In open battle Croesus' forces had to retreat because the horses in his army could not

IN THE BALANCE

The formidable Sardinian fort, a source of food and water, was overtaken by Persia and the Selucids.

stand to be in the presence of the camels of the Persians. Following fast on the Lydian army, the Persian King Cyrus reached the capital city but was frustrated when he arrived there. The Lydians had retreated into their citadel, locking it up tight, fearful of nothing. It seemed that the fortress was unassailable. For two weeks the Persian army sat below while trying to map out a strategy to break the stalemate. Finally, Cyrus offered a generous reward to any in his army who could find a way to take the city.

That night one of his soldiers watched as a careless Lydian sentry dropped his helmet over the wall. The sentry squeezed through one of the many crevices that had developed in the then already crumbling wall, carefully maneuvered down to his helmet, picked it up and returned. Quickly a small force of Persians followed the same path taken by the sentry. Incredibly, when they reached the wall everyone was asleep, the wall unguarded. The Lydians thought themselves so safe as to not stay awake. While the city and the sentries slept, the Persian army poured into the streets, easily taking it before reinforcements from the Lydian countryside could reach in time to save the kingdom.

This foolishness did not happen just once, but twice. When Antiochus III, leading an army of the Seleucid Empire, came in 218 B.C.. to conquer the city, the exact same thing happened with precisely the same results. The cracks of the wall were observed when a sentry slipped through them, his path was marked by the Persians, and again, the walls were breached by the Seleucids, only to find the sentries gone or asleep. Once more the people of Sardis slept through the night rather than be on guard, fooled into thinking that their security was assured.

Impoverished Pretension

After suffering conquest twice and having its treasury looted, the wealth of Sardis became nothing but a legend. It still took pride in its past glory although time and fortune had been unkind. The walls were standing but continued crumbling. The gold mines were depleted, the gold dust in the Pactolus replaced with nothing but sand. So poverty stricken was the city that in 17 A.D. when hit by a devastating earthquake, it could not recover without help. The Emperor Tiberius remitted taxes for five years and made a substantial grant to help rebuild the city. The gift allowed the city to regain much of the appearance of its past splendor but never to the degree it had once known. With its glorious past still the thing of legend, persisting to New Testament days was the saying "to capture the acropolis of Sardis" to describe doing the impossible.

Despite the efforts to restore the city, it was a caricature. Sir William Ramsay writes, "It was the city whose name was almost synonymous with pretensions unjustified, promise unfulfilled, appearance without reality, confidence that heralded ruin. Reputed to be an impregnable fortress, it had repeatedly fallen short of reputation, and ruined those who trusted in it. Croesus had fancied he could sit safe in the great fortress, but his enemy advanced straight upon it and carried it by assault before the strength of the Lydian land was collected."[28]

Religion in Sardis

Sardis was a center for the worship of Dionysius whose father was Zeus and his mother a human named Semele. According to myth, Dionysius was removed from his mother while she was pregnant. Zeus then carried the unborn infant in his thigh until birth. Followers said that Dionysius had been twice born. The two festivals in his name were associated with vernal and autumnal equinox. With that there were themes of resurrection.

Kent Ulery notes that the followers of Dionysius preferred mystery, helped along by healthy servings of alcohol. But they also worked themselves up into frenzies with wild singing and dancing. The festivals could become rowdy affairs with sacrificial animals dismembered, their blood drunk. The worship frequently degenerated into orgies.[29] This led to Sardis being widely known for immoral lifestyles, the people bent on seeking pleasure and creature comforts as they lived in overall decadence. In an age of low morals, Sardis was seen as a place where the most extreme behaviors were commonplace, not only tolerated but also encouraged. As a result its name was spoken of with contempt.

It is no surprise that part of the reason that the city had degenerated was the impotence of religion to have any moderating influence. A large synagogue was there, the ruins of which can be seen today. Although the Jews had allied themselves against the Christians in other cities, apparently the Christian witness was virtually non-existent so as not to stir up any notice, let alone persecution. Coupled with that was the decadence of the Jewish religion in Sardis, whose followers hardly cared about the purity of their own worship, let alone perceiving a threat to it.

---

[28]*Ramsay, 404*
[29]*Ulery, 70-71*

The temple of Cybele was physically adjoined to the church building in Sardis. Cybele was reputed to be the mother of the gods, whose worship rivaled Dionysius for wild decadence. The church being in such close proximity to a heathen temple like Cybele was inconceivable anywhere else. But even the extreme pagan worshippers found the Christians to be no irritation. For their part, the Christians seemed to take a "let's all just get along" approach to living in Sardis. It may be that they caused no concern because they were willing participants in the behaviors of the Sardinians. Or perhaps they were among the first to believe that all paths lead to the same god. "As long as you're sincere…" the mantra of those who believe getting along is more important than standing for something. It is a reminder of the epitaph the writer of Judges gave at the end of his book after recounting the sad history of Israel after claiming the Promised Land, " … everyone did as he saw fit" (21:20).

A synagogue courtyard in Sardis, where the practice of Judaism was depraved and impure.

Such was the state of things in the Sardis church. No heresies concerned it, no persecution besieged it. The Christians were there but had the earth opened up and swallowed their church building, it is doubtful that anyone would have noticed. Nor would it seem that the Christians would have been terribly concerned either. It was quiet in Sardis for the Christians. But cemeteries are quiet, too.

To the angel of the church in Sardis write: These are the words of Him who holds the seven spirits of God and the seven stars. I know your deeds; you have a reputation of being alive, but you are dead (Revelation 3:1).

Unlike the letters to the other churches there is no commendation of any kind given to Sardis. That alone was a stinging rebuke.

The message is direct and startling. This was not a church that was compromised, troubled, suffering internal dissension, financially at the brink or going through a bad time. It was a dead church. Like the city of Sardis, it was pretentious without substance. It had a hollow reputation for being alive. Probably they congratulated themselves that the church was a beehive of activity, could highlight wonderful accomplishments being made by the church. Someone stepping into one of its meetings for the first time might very well be impressed by all the commotion, all the noise, all the action. So the reputation was that this was an energized place. Actually, it was more like a disembodied echo that sounds but is no longer connected with a living being.

One of the great lessons Elijah had to learn was that God is not always in the dramatic. Having come from the spectacular moment on Carmel when fire descended and the people made a mass profession of faith, he might have felt that the new norm for God was to overwhelm the opposition. After running from Queen Jezebel he was alone and deeply depressed. Seeking God's voice, he listened for God in the fire, the wind and the earthquake only to find He was silent in all of these (1 Kings 19:11-13). It was in the silence that God spoke.

Special effects can awe the crowds but the watchers walk away unchanged. Thrilling performances will be admired and likely remembered and talked about, but it doesn't mean that the listener will examine his life. Churches that seek to emulate the excitement of a sports event rarely see that translate into changes in lifestyle. When the church seeks Hollywood instead of the Holy Spirit, it can make a splash but its influence is as short-lived as a ripple in the pond. That was where Sardis was. All the noise and excitement died away along with any positive effect when the doors were closed and everyone went home.

The church likely gave lip service to its doctrine. A doctrine understood but not practiced is nothing more than a whimsical idea. It likely sang of a resurrected Christ while living as if He was still dead. They may have continually crowded people into the meetings where they laughed and fellowshipped and encouraged so that it was certain it was meeting needs. But a church that does no more than that is more of a club or a substitute for the neighborhood bar than a place of worship and service.

Signs of a Dying Church

William Barclay gives several signs of a dying church that are worth noting with further comment.[30]

1. A church is in danger of death when it begins to worship its own past. The people of Sardis were rightly proud of their past history as a kingdom. But the greatness of the past was nothing more than a tale told with little affect on the present. Christianity can be wiped out by a single generation abandoning the faith. Although history encourages and challenges, past battles fought do not replace the need to meet the enemy and secure victory in the present day. The battle must be constantly joined, victory not assumed because of what happened yesterday.

---

[30]Barclay, 73-74

2. The church is in danger when it is more concerned with forms than with life. The children of Israel were given the ceremonies and the Tabernacle with its furnishings to serve as tutors about their relationship with God. These were important when their lessons were learned but they were never meant to be ends in themselves. The problem is that people find it easier to understand what they hold in their hands. But the object can become the focus and the meaning behind it forgotten or eclipsed. That is exactly what happened. The danger in the present is the same. A rite, a ceremony, a procedure can be observed flawlessly but never teach the lesson intended. A dying church has lost the meaning of its ritual and practice.

3. A church is in danger of death when it loves systems more than it loves Jesus. The Church, as well as individual denominations, has to perform efficiently. That is simply good stewardship. In the present day there is a great danger, however, in trying to use a business model of management and organization as the template to define and handle the living Body of Christ. Its life cannot be reduced to forms or procedures. Its government acts as a clear channel to advance the mission of Christ, not a maze to test the people within it. Accountability is needed but layers of bureaucracy can strangle Spirit-led initiative and kill a church.

4. A church is in danger of death when it is more concerned with material than spiritual things. The problem with obtaining anything tangible is that care and concern must be giving to keeping and maintaining it. It is wonderful to be a homeowner, but anyone who has owned a house knows that time and effort must be given to upkeep and protection of the home or the investment will

be lost. He also knows that in owning a home, he is not free to pick up and move when he pleases. The home gives him security but it comes at a cost. The church is no different. The more it acquires, the more it must devote to maintaining and protecting it.

Most people and churches can balance the need to take care of what is theirs with the rest of life. But there are always those individuals who are not guardians of their homes but slaves to them. The church as well, when it concerns itself too deeply with its own maintenance, its own assets, can find that it has lost its fervor for the things of God as it attends to the gain and storage of mammon.

Wake up! Strengthen what remains and is about to die, for I have found your deeds unfinished in the sight of my God. Remember, therefore, what you have received and heard; hold it fast, and repent. But if you do not wake up, I will come like a thief, and you will not know at what time I will come to you (Revelation 3:2-3).

With the memory of sleeping guards on the ramparts that allowed the enemy to enter its fortress, the command "Wake up!" had special relevance to the church in Sardis. The King James Version translates that same command, "Be watchful." That may be a better rendering because waking up is done in an instant. The tense of the verb means to watch and keep on watching. Had there been watchfulness when Cyrus and Antiochus attacked, Sardis would not have fallen nor would ruin and carelessness have become the legacy of the city.

The Lord speaks of finding their deeds unfinished. The word for "found" is eureka, a word coined by Archimedes when he stepped into the bathtub and noticed water rising, helping to crystallize the discovery that the amount of mass in water must have an equal amount of water displaced as a result. It was a word meant for a happy and fortuitous discovery. In using this word, it seems that the Lord was looking expectantly to find something exciting. But in the case of Sardis, it was a most disappointing discovery. Instead of finding a Spirit-filled church, well winning its town to Christ, the Lord found one that was gasping its last breath.

The solution to this sorry state is given: Remember. It is to be a continuous action. Remember and keep on remembering. Keep ever before you what the story of the gospel is, how Christ came into the world, suffered and died for it. Remember how He tore loose the chains of death in glorious resurrection. Remember how the Holy Spirit came in power at Pentecost, and thus, filled with His power and presence, the witnesses carried this good news across the known world and beyond. Remember the day when the gospel came to Sardis and some of you were amazed, intrigued, troubled until you could resist Him no longer and knelt at His bleeding feet. Keep thinking of what it was like when others came seeking, when you saw people stop what they were doing to listen to you

Cybele, reputed to be the mother of the gods, whose worship rivaled that of Dionysius in decadence.

tell of a Savior and they, too, found Him. Keep remembering, people of Sardis.

The remembering will inevitably lead to repentance. Step back and look at yourselves. Is this what God destined you to be? Is this the witness that your city needs? How are you different? Go back from this place of death to the place where you found life. Turn around because there is no future along this path.

In almost every movie produced nowadays about some future apocalypse the filmmakers show familiar landmarks in ruins. Here is the tilting arm of the Statue of Liberty nearly buried in sand. There is the Eiffel Tower, little more than its base still intact. Over here is Big Ben and the Houses of Parliament with gaping holes. All speak of utter destruction, but these landmarks recall that there was once a great civilization here. Remember what you used to be, church of Sardis, because in the present your landscape is littered with ruins, the mocking remains of past greatness.

If you fail to turn back, then the Lord says, "I will come as a thief." Your forefathers failed to realize their peril and while an army could not assail your defenses, a few men breached the walls and brought your city down in defeat. They sneaked in at night and stole your liberty away. I will come, Christ says, and all for you will be lost if you do not repent.

Yet you have a few people in Sardis who have not soiled their clothes. They will walk with me, dressed in white, for they are worthy. The one who is victorious will, like them, be dressed in white. I will never blot out the name of that person from the book of life, but will acknowledge that name before my Father and His angels. Whoever has ears, let them hear what the Spirit says to the churches (Revelation 3:4-6).

Fortunately, all was not lost in Sardis. There were still a few who had not surrendered to the culture, had not compromised but had kept themselves clean. When things look bleak, it is too easy to throw hands in the air and declare that all is lost. Elijah did that, feeling that he was the sole faithful servant of God (1 Kings 19:18).

IN THE BALANCE

But as the Lord reminded Elijah, in every age and in every land He will always have His witness.

When under communist rule, the leaders of Albania boasted that they had succeeded in erasing any remnants of Christianity within its borders. However, when the Iron Curtain fell in 1989, one of the poignant scenes soon afterwards on a TV news programs was a single Albanian man standing in front of a pathetic silver celluloid Christmas tree. With no musical accompaniment, he sang a traditional Christmas carol heralding the birth of Christ. The claim of Christianity's demise was false. Christ continued to live in a remnant of the Albanian people.

White Garments

In underscoring the faithfulness of the few, the Lord made use once again of an image familiar to them because the city was still famous for its woolen garments.

The appearance of garments was very important then as it is now. In ancient times, wearing soiled garments eliminated people from entering worship services. Dirty garments were also the sign of grief and like sackcloth and ashes, a sign of repentance. Condemned criminals, to show their guilt, also wore them. But the faithful of Sardis were not required to wear soiled clothing. Instead, they would be dressed in white.

Being dressed in white had several uses well known to people who lived in the Roman Empire.

1. When a general returned victoriously from a key battle, a Triumph was ordered through the streets of Rome. The general was arrayed in white to show that he was honored for having fought for his country and prevailed. The victorious of Sardis would be honored for having fought their own bitter battle on behalf of their Lord.

2. Angels are portrayed in Scripture as wearing white (Matthew 28:3). White, then, was appropriate for those in

the presence of God. So these of Sardis would be properly attired to dwell in God's presence.

3. Later in Revelation the redeemed are in white, having washed their robes in the blood of the Lamb (Revelation 7:14). It was the blood of Christ that allowed entrance, the assurance that the blood covered all of a person's sins. It is rewarded not because they did anything to deserve it, but because they remained faithful.

4. On the day of their baptism, believers were dressed in white to symbolize their new life in Christ. So the white raiment testified to their inner life of salvation.

The Book of Life

Jesus promised anyone found worthy that "I will never blot out his name in the book of life." Curiously, there is almost no mention of names being entered into the book of life but rather to names being blotted out. To have a name blotted out was to signify that person's eternal death. From the context of the Scriptures where it is mentioned, the removal of a name comes from a person's rebellion and disobedience to God. It raises questions about the claims to unconditional eternal security with regard to salvation. The testimony of the Bible is that there was a point when the name was removed, even though it was previously recorded. This squares with the teaching found in Ezekiel 33:12, 13 that says, "Therefore, son of man, say to your people, 'If someone who is righteous disobeys, that person's former righteousness will count for nothing. And if someone who is wicked repents, that person's former wickedness will not bring condemnation. The righteous person who sins will not be allowed to live even though they were formerly righteous.' If I tell a righteous person that they will surely live, but then they trust in their righteousness and do evil, none of the righteous things that person has done will be remembered; they will die for the evil they have done."

IN THE BALANCE

The idea of a registration book was familiar to the ancient people. The Bible tells of such a registry for the Jewish people (Psalm 69:28; Isaiah 4:3). In Sardis, at the death of a prominent person, it was the practice to read out their names for their praiseworthy lives, an honor that Sardisians would have cherished. On the other side, the ancient Greeks removed names from their registry of any who had committed treason or been condemned for their crimes. It was as if they never existed. For the Christian, to have his name in the Book of Life is to be assured that God owns him. To have it removed is not only a death sentence, but also a mark of the deepest shame.

The church in Sardis is an example of what happens when believers fail to be salt and light where they are. Christianity was never meant to be a philosophy, a set of teachings or a code of conduct, although it certainly encompasses all of these. God meant for the church to be the body of Christ in the world, His representative, His witness. To fail to do so is to be dead.

Discussion Questions

1. The city of Sardis fell twice to invaders because they failed to watch. What lesson is this to the believer?

2. Why was the lack of persecution in Sardis a bad thing?

3. The author says about the church in Sardis, "had the earth opened up and swallowed their church building, it is doubtful that anyone would have noticed." Why or why not would this be said about your church?

4. Is there a time in the life of your church when it had a greater witness than it does now? If so, what changed?

5. In many places in the world, Christians constitute a despised and persecuted minority. How can you support them?

Personal Reflection

1. Is it apparent to others that you live for Christ? Why or why not?

2. How do you define a meaningful worship experience at church?

3. Read again the signs of a dying church. Now compile your own list of what it looks like when a Christian's spiritual life is dying.

4. The church in Sardis is told to remember as the pathway back to vitality. Is there a time you can remember when your spiritual life was more alive than it is today? How do you now recover what was lost?

5. Describe what it means to you to someday receive white robes from the Lord.

Revelation 3:7-13
To the Church in Philadelphia

7 "To the angel of the church in Philadelphia write:

These are the words of him who is holy and true, who holds the key of David. What he opens no one can shut, and what he shuts no one can open. 8 I know your deeds. See, I have placed before you an open door that no one can shut. I know that you have little strength, yet you have kept my word and have not denied my name. 9 I will make those who are of the synagogue of Satan, who claim to be Jews though they are not, but are liars—I will make them come and fall down at your feet and acknowledge that I have loved you. 10 Since you have kept my command to endure patiently, I will also keep you from the hour of trial that is going to come on the whole world to test the inhabitants of the earth.

11 I am coming soon. Hold on to what you have, so that no one will take your crown. 12 The one who is victorious I will make a pillar in the temple of my God. Never again will they leave it. I will write on them the name of my God and the name of the city of my God, the new Jerusalem, which is coming down out of heaven from my God; and I will also write on them my new name. 13 Whoever has ears, let them hear what the Spirit says to the churches."

IN THE BALANCE

PHILADELPHIA:
Standing Firm

— Revelation 3:7-13

D uring the First World War, the Germans bombed London using fleets of zeppelins. Because of its location in the downtown area of the city, the leaders at St. Paul's Cathedral realized that if a bomb should hit the church, the grand dome could collapse inward, likely destroying the landmark structure. After the war ended in 1918 it was decided to fill the great columns that supported the dome with concrete in case another conflict should arise and the city come under attack again. Sadly, it did a little over 20 years later when in the Battle of Britain the German Luftwaffe made countless raids on the city, leveling whole sections and leaving thousands dead and wounded. Night after night the planes came, leaving the city illuminated from the flames of burning buildings. Some bombs hit the great cathedral causing damage, but it survived because its fortified pillars weathered the withering attacks. Amid the smoke and fire, the dome of St. Paul's stood proud, a symbol of hope during a time of great trial.

Standing through the battle did not begin with St. Paul's Cathedral. The little church in Philadelphia stood tall through the firestorm of persecution.

A Tribute Name

Originally part of the Kingdom of Pergamum, Philadelphia was founded in 189 B.C. by King Eumenes II. He named it Philadelphia, meaning "brotherly love" in honor of his brother and successor, Attalus II. It was fitting to give it this name since the two brothers

PHILADELPHIA: Standing Firm

Ruins of Philadelphia, for centuries a Christian stronghold amid Jewish rejection and Islamic expansion.

were inseparable and unfailingly loyal to each other. The purpose of the city's founding was to spread the Greek language and culture throughout the area. It was, in a secular sense, created with a missionary purpose in mind.

An earthquake destroyed Philadelphia in 17 A.D., the city continuing to suffer aftershocks for many years. Some of the aftershocks were almost as bad as the earthquake itself, causing additional harm to buildings left standing or further wrecking ones previously damaged. The Greek historian Strabo recorded the effects of the earthquake on Philadelphia, " ... Philadelphia ... has not even its walls secure, but they are daily shaken and split in some degree. The people continually pay attention to earth tremors and plan their buildings with these factors in mind ... for the walls never cease being cracked, and different parts of the city are constantly suffering damage. That is why the actual town has few inhabitants, but the majority live as farmers in the countryside, as they have fertile land. But one is surprised even at the few, that they are so fond of the place when they have insecure buildings."[31] Those who stayed in Philadelphia tried to fortify the buildings with additional supports, including gigantic pillars, some of which have survived to the present day.

Following the earthquake, Emperor Tiberius remitted taxes to Philadelphia to assist it in its rebuilding. In gratitude, the town renamed itself Neocaesarea, or "The New Town of Caesar." After Tiberius died, the new name eventually fell into disuse and the old name of Philadelphia was once again used.

In the second century A.D., it was home to Ammia, an outstanding Christian prophetess whose ministry spanned nearly 60 years. The Christian historian Eusebius ranked her with the four daughters of Philip (Acts 21:9), recording that she not only was a staunch witness for the Faith but also had a gift for predicting the future.

Philadelphia continued for centuries as a Christian stronghold even when the rest of the surrounding country fell to Islamic expansion. Although it was besieged many times by Islamic armies, it held strong through the fourteenth century. It finally fell when a Christian army combined with Islamic forces to overwhelm it. Despite this and its location in the Islamic country of Turkey, it continues to the present day to count half of its residents as Christians.

Religion in Philadelphia

Philadelphia was home to a large number of temples to a variety of gods, so much so that it was called "Little Athens." Because it was a grape growing area, it paid special allegiance to Dionysius, the god of the grape. Of particular note, is that when one of the leaders of the city died, his name was carved on one of the pillars in Dionysius' temple.

As in other cities of Asia, there was a significant Jewish presence, one that was violently hostile to the Christian community. In spite

[31]Quoted in Hemer, 156

of the entrenched forces arrayed against it, the Christian church was vibrant, alive in its witness and successful enough to engender persecution from those who were angered by its efforts to win people to Christ.

To the angel of the church in Philadelphia write: These are the words of Him who is holy and true, who holds the key of David. What He opens no one can shut, and what He shuts no one can open. I know your deeds. See, I have placed before you an open door that no one can shut. I know that you have little strength, yet you have kept my word and have not denied my name (Revelation 3:7-8).

The letter to the church in Philadelphia contains no words of condemnation; instead it breathes encouragement in every line.

The Lord identified Himself as the one who is holy and true. Ironically, the Roman emperors referred to themselves as holy but even a cursory examination of their lives shows that the term did not hold much meaning. It would be difficult to find any vice in use at the time that wasn't a well-known and accepted practice of the emperors. Reclaiming the term as God meant it to be, Jesus called Himself holy, an attribute that is innate to God alone.

Calling Himself "true" does not mean so much of the opposite of false but rather genuine and authentic. It also has the Hebrew idea of faithfulness, as in a true friend. To the church in Philadelphia, betrayed by the Jewish community, the reminder that Christ remained faithful to them must have been a wonderful word of consolation.

The words of Joseph M. Scriven would have been sung heartily by the church in Philadelphia, especially the second verse:

Have we trials and temptations?
Is there trouble anywhere?
We should never be discouraged—
Take it to the Lord in prayer.
Can we find a friend so faithful,
Who will all our sorrows share?

Jesus knows our every weakness;
Take it to the Lord in prayer.[32]

Jesus used an Old Testament reference for Himself. He is the one " … who holds the key of David. What He opens no one can shut, and what He shuts, no one can open." These words first appear in Isaiah 22:22 in reference to Eliakim, the steward of the king's palace.

"I will place on his shoulder the key to the house of David; what he opens no one can shut, and what he shuts no one can open." The steward was the one who allowed people in to see the king. Christ took up this image, applying it to refer to Himself as the only entry into the Father's presence. It is reminiscent of John 14:6, "I am the way and the truth and the life. No one comes to the Father except through me."

An Open Door

After assuring the Philadelphians that He knows their deeds, Christ told them that in His authority as the one who holds the key, He has placed before them an open door. Too weak to open it themselves, the Almighty God holds it open for them. Just as reassuring is that the door the Lord closes cannot be forcefully opened by someone else. The tense of the verb indicates that it is not only open but it is staying open and what He shuts stays shut.

Exactly what is the purpose of the open door? Some have suggested that it is the open door of salvation. Others think it is for prayer. Still others think it is for their entry into the presence of God. Given the city's missionary past for spreading Hellenism to that region, the open door also likely stands for their opportunity to go out into the world with the gospel. It certainly is not one of escape from the world and all its troubles. It is one that opens the Christian up to larger opportunity.

When the time neared for Hong Kong to be reunited with Mainland

---

[32] *As found in "Timeless Truths" http://library.timelesstruths.org/music/What_a_Friend_We_Have_in_Jesus/ accessed on April 3, 2013*

China in 1996, many feared that the communist government would close Christian work in the city. But the Chinese Christians in Hong Kong had an entirely different view. For many years the door had been closed to them to go into China to share the gospel. With the reunification, they now had an open door to travel freely into mainland China both to encourage the struggling church within that great country as well as share the gospel. The relatively small numbers of believers of the church in Hong Kong never was a concern. The opportunity eclipsed any thoughts of being intimidated.

Christ recognized the weakness of the church, yet the people had been steadfast nonetheless. Theirs had not been a silent witness but a constant testimony. It was like a bugle clearly sounding over the background din of life in Philadelphia. All Christians in these days understood what speaking out about their faith would mean. But it was not done to gain approval points or to even make the Christian faith more palatable. They shared because they must. The prophet Jeremiah spoke the irresistible need to witness: "But if I say, 'I will not mention His word or speak anymore in His name,' His word is in my heart like a fire, a fire shut up in my bones. I am weary of holding it in; indeed, I cannot" (20:9).

Jesus said that they had "kept my word." The word "keep" is repeated in verse 10, where it means to preserve. Here it speaks of obedience. In essence, Christ is saying, "Because you have kept my commandments, I will keep you through the trials." Obedience is proper in and of itself but it also allows for God to bless in ways He cannot if a person chooses his own path. Obedience positions us in the place where blessing can occur. Oecuminius wrote, "by keeping the faith of Christ, it rose above its own strength, as one undaunted to live among those who trouble the faithful."[33]

I will make those who are of the synagogue of Satan, who claim to be Jews though they are not, but are liars—I will make them come and fall down at your feet and acknowledge that I have loved you. Since you have

---

[33] *Ancient Christian Commentary on Scripture, Volume XII, 45*

Destruction of the Temple in Jerusalem, A.D. 70, a catastrophe to early Christians as well as to Jews.

*kept my command to endure patiently, I will also keep you from the hour
of trial that is going to come on the whole world to test the inhabitants of
the earth* (Revelation 3:9,10).

As in other cities, the people of Philadelphia faced fierce opposition from the established Jewish community. When Christianity first started it was seen as a part of Judaism, because many of the early converts were almost exclusively Jewish. It was common for Jewish Christians to attend the synagogue where Christianity was openly discussed and then to attend a house church for further study. But when Christianity opened its doors to Gentiles and Gentiles enthusiastically flocked into the church, the ties to traditional Judaism were strained. Then the Gentiles were allowed to bypass established and valued Jewish rites, resulting in divergent paths taking the two religions further apart. An attempt to reconcile the two and perhaps keep Christianity in the fold of Judaism was the teaching of the Judaizers who believed Gentiles should practice the rites of Judaism. The most contentious issue was male circumcision. The church leadership had freed the Gentile believers from observing any of the old Jewish practices with the exception of instructing them to live sexually pure lives and not eat meat offered to idols or that had blood in it. Contradicting this, the Judaizers were a destabilizing influence in the Christian church. The division between traditional Judaism and Christianity was now further splintered by the addition of the Judaizers, who continued to observe all the Jewish law while actively advocating that Gentile believers do the same. This resulted in considerable confusion among the believers. And Paul, who before his conversion had been a model Jew, took up the cause of Gentile believers being freed from the burden of Jewish rites.

While major theological issues were at the crux of the matter, there were practical issues as well. The Jewish community in Asia had won considerable concessions for its religious practices from the Greek and then the Roman rulers of the land. These amounted to a number of time honored legal protections as well as freedom to opt out of civic activities that were part of the culture but offensive to the Jews. As the Christian religion gained prominence, the Christian Jews naturally expected that they would receive the same sheltering protection since they were Hebrews by birth. And by extension, the Gentile believers, who shared the same beliefs on many identical and essential issues, sought protection as well. But the Jewish community that might have tolerated the Christian Jews would not consider extending anything to the Gentiles who were not even observing their laws. Instead, their anger over theological issues was stoked further by the efforts to seek the protections offered to them by the Roman government. Their answer was not to extend a hand of protection but to vehemently attack the Christian church; doing all they could to distance themselves from what had now become a distinct and separate religion from Judaism.

The depth of Jewish resentment can be seen in the Benediction of Minim, which Rabin Gamaliel requested Samuel ha-Katan to write: "For the apostates let there be no hope. And let the arrogant government be speedily uprooted in our days. Let the *nozerim* and the *minim* be destroyed in a moment. And let them be blotted out of the Book of Life and not be inscribed together with the righteous. Blessed art Thou, O Lord, who humblest the arrogant."[34] The word *minim* was equivalent to "Nazarenes," one of the early names by which Christians were known. This benediction was formulated in 90 A.D. and would have been in wide circulation by the time Revelation was written. In isolation, one benediction would not mean that much but it is a barometer of how bitter the feelings were from the Jewish community toward the Christians.

Anger at the Judaizers in particular became a frequently expressed sentiment early on. Paul railed against them often. An example of this has Paul speaking about their insistence that Christians be circumcised. "Watch out for those dogs, those evildoers, those mutilators of the flesh" (Philippians 3:2). The Jews commonly referred to Gentiles as dogs. For Paul to use that phrase to describe the

---

[34] Found at http://www.jewishvirtuallibrary.org/jsource/judaica/ejud_0002_0003_0_02999.html, accessed on March 7, 2013

Judaizers was highly inflammatory. Other such warnings and pronouncements are sprinkled throughout the New Testament. Even though rhetoric in these days was often stated in the most extreme terms, it was taken quite seriously nonetheless.

From the Lord's point of view, the split and resulting resentment was never His intention. He said, "Do not think that I have come to

Christians in Philadelphia lived obediently and with patient endurance.

IN THE BALANCE

abolish the Law or the Prophets; I have not come to abolish them but to fulfill them" (Matthew 5:17). God's purpose was that Judaism would be completed by accepting Christ as the Messiah, the full expression of God's love not only for the Jewish people but all the peoples of the world. When the Jewish religion as a whole rejected Christ and then turned against His followers, it was not a protection of their civil rights but rebellion against the will of God.

The church in Philadelphia felt the full force of Jewish rejection and vengefulness. Jesus referred to them as the "synagogue of Satan" because of their rebellion and attacks upon His people. The synagogue should have been a sanctuary for the people of God. Instead it was the most dangerous place in the city.

In His indictment of them, Jesus charged that they "claim to be Jews though they are not, but are liars." By this time it was already being taught that the promises and covenants that were made with the Hebrew people had passed to those who were in Christ. Paul wrote, "A person is not a Jew who is one only outwardly, nor is circumcision merely outward and physical. No, a person is a Jew who is one inwardly; and circumcision is circumcision of the heart, by the Spirit, not by the written code. Such a person's praise is not from other people, but from God" (Romans 2:28, 29). By their rebellion, the ones born as Hebrews had ceased being Jews in God's sight. And those Christians who asserted what Paul wrote only added fuel to the fire.

Bowing Down to the Beaten Down

The consequence of the synagogue members rejecting and persecuting the Christians was a total reversal of what they had come to expect. Jews in this day were taught that in the Messianic kingdom the people of other nations would come and bow at their feet. But Jesus told the Philadelphians that it was the Jews who so fiercely opposed them that would bow at the feet of these humble Christians. The usage of the term in Revelation of "bow down" always indicates a voluntary action. What it means is that the Jews who so opposed them in the Day of Judgment will realize the offense they have committed. It will be their time to be humble, to seek forgiveness from those they have harmed.

The action of bowing down is not just as an apology but also in recognition that the beleaguered Christians have actually been the true servants of the Lord. For Christians who labor in countries or in situations where they are subject to gross abuses of power by those over them, this is a word of consolation. Told they are enemies of God, it will be seen that they are His friends. Power does not equal righteousness, nor popular approval the favor of God.

Kept

The Philadelphians handled their entire affliction by living obediently with patient endurance. The endurance spoken of is not an effort to lay low so as to be unnoticed, nor is it to withdraw until the storm passes. It is the kind of endurance that holds the ground in the face of the foes attacking. Think of it as the difference between a fearful soldier huddling deep within a foxhole and another one manning his post as the enemy advances. For the Philadelphians this meant to steadfastly refuse to bow down to the statue of Tiberius and proclaim him as lord. It meant that in a city full of temples, despite what their former lives had dictated or their families and friends urged, they would not go inside to offer a prayer "just in case." Nor was it to hide away an idol to offer a sacrifice in secret as a backup plan if the gospel somehow failed them. Instead, it meant to burn the bridges that led back to their old life, to take a course that to those who were not believers seemed totally out of touch with reality.

For their obedience and steadfastness, Christ promised to keep them from the hour of trial. It is uncertain as to what this hour of trial is because the wording does not make the hour of trial sound exclusive to Christians. History tells us that the persecutions that were then just getting traction would become increasingly more widespread, more intense and more deadly. It may be that this persecution, which was a trial to the Christians, was as much a trial to the rest of the civilized world as well.

IN THE BALANCE

When the Nazis conquered the European continent they not only subjugated the citizens of the defeated country, but they began systematic purges of the undesirable people who lived within the borders. Not only were Jews taken but also Gypsies, Slavic peoples, homosexuals, Jehovah's Witnesses, political enemies, church leaders or any who would dare speak out against them. While many people were passive about the removal of their neighbors, there were others who were deeply troubled and took action to hide or smuggle people to safety. Even though these rescuers were not part of the targeted populations, they were distressed by the Nazi actions. Many paid with their lives or were ruined as a result. Later, when the allies invaded Europe, they retook the conquered territories from the Nazis. But in doing so, they laid waste to whole cities and the countryside. The country suffered in a whole new way even though they were not specifically targeted. It is not hard to imagine that in a similar way, non-Christians within the Empire, who were deeply troubled by their government's actions, sought to protect or help the Christians and may have suffered as a result. When a nation sets itself to commit evil, the negative effects are not neatly contained within one segment of the population. The infection poisons the whole body. That may be what Jesus is referring to about an hour of trial for the whole world.

The good news was that the Lord promised to keep the suffering people of Philadelphia. Keeping them did not mean keeping all they had. They would be kept even though their jobs might be lost. They would be kept although their possessions might be confiscated. They would be kept although they might see their family members taken away. They would be kept although they might be standing in an arena somewhere waiting for the wild beasts to be set loose upon them. They would be kept because at the moment of unimaginable tragedy, the breadth of God's grace would be in full operation. The God who gave them grace to live would be present to give them grace to die.

I am coming soon. Hold on to what you have, so that no one will take your crown. The one who is victorious I will make a pillar in the temple of my God. Never again will they leave it. I will write on them the name of my God and the name of the city of my God, the new Jerusalem, which is coming down out of heaven from my God; and I will also write on them my new name. Whoever has ears, let them hear what the Spirit says to the churches (Revelation 3:11-13).

The first generation of Christians fully expected that the Lord would return within their lifetime. Each generation since then has hoped that their age would be the time of the Lord's return. The sense in this passage, however, is that the Lord will not delay His coming beyond the appointed time.

The admonition to hold on or risk losing the crown that is theirs indicates that it could be lost. Cyprian said, "For confession (of Christ) does not make one immune from the snares of the devil. Nor does it defend one who is still placed in the world with a perpetual security against worldly temptations and dangers and onsets and attacks ... Whoever the confessor is, he is not greater or better than Solomon. As long as he walked in the ways of the Lord, so long he retained the grace he had received from his Lord. After he had abandoned the way of the Lord, he lost also the grace of the Lord."[35]

It is not that the crown is so precarious that every bump or jostle would cause it to go tumbling off. But neither should the believer assume that once given, it would always be his regardless of how he lives his life afterwards. Jesus told them to hold on. That implies that not only was it never meant to be lost but also it was never to be taken for granted either. Holding on is not a virtue that elicits boasting but an action needed to survive. Like the person in intensive care that takes one breath after another until the life giving surgery can take place, holding on is not something to boast about. It is the only thing that the patient can do for the healing action to take place. In the command to hold on, it is not self-salvation that is being talked about but standing firm until deliverance comes.

---

[35]*Ancient Christian Commentary on Scripture, Vol. XII, 46*

Pillars in the Temple

Then to the people who knew what it was to run from tumbling buildings in earthquakes and during aftershocks, the Lord promised that the believer will be "a pillar in the temple of my God."

Pillars were functional, the main means of supporting a roof or upper story on a building. They had to be strong not only for themselves, but for all that they supported. The idea relates as well back to the previous verse. The pillar was meant to stand firm even though everything else might crumble around it. The pillar spoke of permanency. John Stott has written, "If, then, we become a pilgrim in this life, we will be a pillar in the next."[36]

The word used for temple signifies the innermost sanctuary of the Temple in Jerusalem, the place where only the priests entered called the Holy Place. By this time, the Temple in Jerusalem lay in ruins, torn down to the ground by the Roman army under Titus in 70 AD. The destruction of the Temple was an unspeakable catastrophe to the Jewish people and by extension, to the Christians as well. For the Jews especially, it was difficult to imagine their life without the Temple, which had been the center of their religious, political, cultural and social lives for centuries. But Jesus told the Philadelphians that the real Temple still stands, not subject to the military might of Rome but always intact as God's possession. And you, faithful Philadelphians, are the pillars in that Temple.

When the believer occupies his place as a pillar in the Temple of God, "never again will he leave it." What a wonderful thought this was to the Philadelphians who had to flee each time the earth tremored in their city. Unlike their hometown of unstable buildings, the unmovable city of God allows its inhabitants to dwell in safety forever.

Finally, the believer is promised, "I will also write on him my new name." In biblical times names were tremendously significant. A baby's name was not just something to call him or chosen because it sounded good. It was a statement about how things were or were

---

[36]Stott, 12

hoped to be. There are several times in the Old Testament that names were given to signify a change in relationship or status. For the believer to be called by a new name establishes a break with the old life with a claim on the new.

A name also speaks of family rights to ownership, authority, and identity. The Scripture says that the new name will be of "my God," the "name of the city of my God" and "my new name." These promise God's holy presence, His dedication to us and His ownership of us. Although broken down in three ways, it is not necessarily true that we will receive three different names but a name that encompasses all these aspects.

In the musical, *Man of LaMancha,* the misguided knight Don Quixote meets a prostitute named Aldonza, calling out to her, "My lady! And I give you a new name – Dulcinea." But things do not go well for her. Later in the play she enters an empty stage following a brutal rape. The knight calls to her, "My lady! Dulcinea!" Recoiling in rage, she screams out to him, "Don't call me a lady. I was born in a ditch by a mother who left me there, naked and cold and too hungry to cry. I never blamed her. I'm sure she left hoping I'd have the good sense to die. Look at me. I'm no lady. I'm only a kitchen slut, reeking with sweat. A strumpet men use and forget. Don't call me Dulcinea. I am only Aldonza and I am nothing at all!" Cloaked in shame, racked by guilt, with no shred of decency left, she then runs off into the darkness.

The knight calls out, "But you are my lady, Dulcinea!"

As the curtain rises on the last act the knight lies dying, heartbroken, condemned as a crazed outcast. To the bed comes a beautiful lady, exquisitely dressed. She kneels by his bed to pray and then he opens his eyes. "Who are you?" he asks.

Standing erect, she answers, "My name? My name is Dulcinea!"

On that last day when the faithful stand with their triumphant Lord, we shall say that we were not what we once were but we are now known by the new name given us by Christ.

IN THE BALANCE

Discussion Questions

1. What door is open for your church's ministry?

2. The friction between the Jewish community and the first century church produced bitter feelings. Did the Christians handle things in the best way? Was conflict inevitable?

3. Given Christ's words to the Philadelphian Christians, how should we act toward the persecuted Christians around the world?

4. In today's world, what examples can you think of where the evil acts of some cause the large scale suffering of not just their named enemies, but of the country itself?

5. It is not unusual to hear one of the local church leaders referred to as a "pillar of the church." How does that term compare with what is said to the believers in Philadelphia?

Personal Reflection

1. What does it mean to you that Christ says that He can open and close doors that no one else can?

2. The Philadelphian Church spoke out in witness despite all the opposition against it. How does that compare with your commitment to be a witness?

3. The believers in Philadelphia had no back up plan in case Christianity failed them. How do you show that same level of confidence?

4. The author says, "The God who gave them grace to live, would be present to give them grace to die." What does that mean to you?

5. With all the uncertainty in life, describe how the promise sounds, given to faithful believers, that in God's eternal Temple the child of God "never again will he leave it."

IN THE BALANCE

MACEDONIA

BULGARIA

Black Sea

Sea of Marmara

N

Aegean Sea

TURKEY

PERGAMUM

THYATIRA

SARDIS

PHILADELPHIA

GREECE

SMYRNA

ATHENS

EPHESUS

LAODICEA

Pelopónnisos

Náxos

Rhodes

Revelation 3:14-22
To the Church in Laodicea

14 *"To the angel of the church in Laodicea write:*

These are the words of the Amen, the faithful and true witness, the ruler of God's creation. 15 I know your deeds, that you are neither cold nor hot. I wish you were either one or the other! 16 So, because you are lukewarm—neither hot nor cold—I am about to spit you out of my mouth. 17 You say, 'I am rich; I have acquired wealth and do not need a thing.' But you do not realize that you are wretched, pitiful, poor, blind and naked. 18 I counsel you to buy from me gold refined in the fire, so you can become rich; and white clothes to wear, so you can cover your shameful nakedness; and salve to put on your eyes, so you can see.

19 Those whom I love I rebuke and discipline. So be earnest and repent. 20 Here I am! I stand at the door and knock. If anyone hears my voice and opens the door, I will come in and eat with that person, and they with me.

21 To the one who is victorious, I will give the right to sit with me on my throne, just as I was victorious and sat down with my Father on his throne. 22 Whoever has ears, let them hear what the Spirit says to the churches."

LAODICEA:
Lukewarm and Loving It

— Revelation 3:14-22

I magine a man going for a checkup with his doctor to complain about what he thinks are some minor health difficulties. Following numerous lab tests, the doctor enters the room. The news is not good.

"Mr. Smith, I tried to warn you that if you did not change your lifestyle, you would face serious health concerns. I'm afraid I was right. The symptoms you complained about are from the XYZ virus. We have no cure for it. Your health will continue to decline. You will never be better than you are right now."

"But I'm wealthy."

"That doesn't matter."

"I wear the best clothes."

"That won't help you, either."

"I have gotten along with everyone. I have no enemies."

"That is irrelevant."

"I've lived a pretty good life. I could have been better but I could have been worse. I can think of a hundred guys who behaved worse than me. If anyone should be sick it ought to be one of them."

"You're missing the point. You are where you are because you not only did a lot of things wrong but you didn't do what was right."

A City of Wealth and Luxury

The city of Laodicea was originally named Diospolis or the City of Zeus. It was rebuilt by King Antiochus II and named after his wife, Laodice. Its name literally means "justice of the people." Its two more famous neighbors, the cities of Colossae and Hierapolis, over-shadowed it. Nearly destroyed in the Mithridatic Wars, it recovered quickly under Roman rule.

It eventually grew to be an impressive city with over 200,000 people. Amenities included a circus that could seat 30,000 people along with three theaters.

In 60 A.D. a massive earthquake completely leveled Laodicea but when Rome offered financial assistance to rebuild it, the inhabitants refused, relying instead on their own considerable resources. The citizenry was very proud of this, resulting in plaques scattered throughout the city with the Latin words, *et ton idion,* "from their own resources."

The source of that wealth was threefold.

First, Laodicea was a major banking center. Some of the wealthiest families in the ancient world lived there including the Zenonid family, the most influential in Asia Minor. Its industries prospered from the investment and development of capital from these individuals, who in turn grew wealthier from the prosperity that attended Laodicean industry.

Second, it was a clothing center. In the countryside around Laodicea a special type of sheep was bred with shiny black wool. Highly valued and extremely expensive, the wool was particularly soft. Around that a booming clothing industry developed. Manufacturers produced both a high end, extremely expensive type of clothing as well as mass-producing cheaper garments. Both were well known and widely used throughout the Roman Empire.

Third, an eye medicine was developed and sold in a tablet form that could be mixed in such a way as to give great relief to those with eye maladies. The medication was known as "Phrygian powder," reputed to have been especially effective in treating eye diseases such as conjunctivitis and slowing the development of cataracts.

Water Problems

There were no good drinkable water sources available to the Laodiceans. Two very different sources were used to bring needed

IN THE BALANCE

Laodicea was a major center for banking and commerce as well as a producer of eye medicine.

water to the city. At Hierapolis, about six miles (10 kilometers) to the north were hot mineral springs. A pipeline was laid between the two cities to carry the calcium carbonate water. The pipes in time became laden with calcium deposits, caked thick on the pipe walls as mute testimony to what was carried in the water. In its transit down the pipes, the water cooled to a tepid temperature by the time it arrived in Laodicea. With a strong smell from the high mineral content and the lukewarmness, drinking the water would often make a person vomit.

The second source of water was from the cold springs located in Colossae, 11 miles (18 kilometers) away. Transported by a great aqueduct, the waters were warmed by the sun and the hot bricks as they reached Laodicea. To live in Laodicea was to become accustomed to lukewarm water. The waters from Colossae were considerably purer than the supply from Hierapolis and much more preferred for drinking.

The waters in Laodicea were known not only for being lukewarm but also for being of poor quality. It is likely that over the years the cleanliness of the pipeline and the aqueduct both suffered. The depth of a person's thirst was what determined whether or not he would risk drinking the water.

Religion in Laodicea

At one point, 2,000 Jewish families were transplanted to Laodicea where they made up a significant part of the population. The lifestyle of the Jews was so lavish that the Jews in Jerusalem complained about their kin who had left Palestine for the luxury and baths of Phrygia. The Jewish historian Josephus notes that this disconnected Jewish community was known for its lax observance of Jewish law and customs and was guilty of syncretism as it absorbed and mixed other religious practices with its own.

The Christian church that grew up in Laodicea seems to have settled into the same kind of religious malaise that the Jewish community exhibited. In the letter to the Laodiceans there is not a single note of praise, no faithful followers are singled out and encouraged. It was a place so worldly, where people lived in such a state of self-satisfaction that the mediocre middle was not only where they found themselves but also where they preferred to be.

Sir William Ramsay notes, "There is no city whose spirit or nature is more difficult to describe than Laodicea. There are no extremes, and hardly any strongly marked features. But in this even balance lies its peculiar character. Those were the qualities that contributed to make it essentially the successful trading city, the city of bankers and finance, which could adapt itself to the needs and wishes of others, ever pliable and accommodating, full of the spirit of compromise."[37] Laodicea personified the old sales adage, "The customer is always right."

The self-centeredness of the church was soon to end. The Stadium

---

[37]Ramsey, 455

of Domitian in Laodicea is the one place that we know for certain that lions were unleashed on Christians, making the message to the Laodiceans all the more urgent. Christ's message to the church no doubt anticipates this with a charge to change. Now is the time to step up and affirm your identity. The day of half-heartedness is over.

To the angel of the church in Laodicea write: These are the words of the Amen, the faithful and true witness, the ruler of God's creation. I know your deeds, that you are neither cold nor hot. I wish you were either one or the other! So, because you are lukewarm—neither hot nor cold—I am about to spit you out of my mouth (Revelation 3:14-16).

To remind the complacent Laodiceans of His authority, Christ used several words to describe Himself.

First, He is the Amen. The word "amen" is used to affirm that something is true or authentic. As William Barclay notes, "To say that Jesus is 'The Amen' is therefore to say that Jesus is the personification and the affirmation of the truth of God."[38] Christ is His own revelation and confirmation of all that God is, all that He does, all that He speaks.

He is the faithful and true witness. Whereas the Laodiceans had given a distorted and diluted picture of Christ and Christianity to their city, the Lord stands against that, defining with crystal clarity who He is and the nature of God's kingdom. His true witness not only speaks of what He says of Himself but of the witness He is now going to bear against the Laodiceans.

He is the source of all creation. Perhaps there were whisperings of Gnosticism in Laodicea, which would have denied that Christ could have had anything directly to do with creation. But the New Testament consistently asserts that Christ did not begin His life in Bethlehem, but He in fact was the eternal Son of God who has always existed. Maintaining that was important. The word used for "source" is the Greek word *arche* from which we get the word

---

[38]*Barclay, 95*

In the Laodicean countryside a special type of sheep was bred to produce shiny black wool. The wool, highly valued and especially soft, became the centerpiece of a booming clothing industry.

archetype, meaning the defining example or epitome of something. In the usage here it means that Christ was not just involved in creation but that it would not have happened at all without Him. Ancient Bible commentator Primaseus said, "He Himself is the Way, who is the fatherland. He Himself is the Author of faith, who is also its fulfiller. He Himself is alpha and omega, He Himself is the beginning whom no one precedes, He Himself is the end whom no one succeeds as ruler."[39]

Neither Hot Nor Cold

The indictment that the Lord pronounces against Laodicea is shocking and damning in the extreme. Had John delivered this letter personally with a hard slap across the face of each person

---

[39]*Ancient Christian Commentary on Scripture, Volume XII, 50*

present who gathered to hear it read, it could not have been a greater blow than what was delivered in this one sentence. The picture portrayed is deliberately graphic, unmistakable in its meaning.

The Greek word for "hot" means boiling; the original for "cold" means icy. In other words, it is better to boil over or to freeze altogether than it is to be in the state you are in.

What exactly was the problem in Laodicea?

1. There was a loss of spiritual sensitivity. When the Spirit of God was moving in their hearts, they just sat there and hoped they'd get over it. When an opportunity came to witness or to speak to the wrong in their community, it became little more than something to be noted, perhaps eliciting a bit of tongue clucking or idly discussed and forgotten. If asked to tell how they were doing in their spiritual lives, if not giving a cursory "I'm just fine," they would have been baffled at the question and what the interrogator was getting at.

2. There was a sense of self-sufficiency. Prayer was perfunctory, mumbled by rote while the mind took faraway journeys; if indeed prayer was uttered in the first place. Heaven held no promise because this world wasn't so bad after all. If something went wrong, someone could be hired or consulted to fix it. The modern equivalent is the church trying to improve itself by first thumbing through a catalog of slick resources to look for a program in a box or engaging a consultant rather than seeking God for His answer. Or the believer going to a support group instead of first going before the Lord. Those things are not wrong in themselves but they are hindrances if the answer is sought in human devices alone or as the first choice instead of in the Word or in prayer. Jesus' words from the Sermon on the Mount set the priority: "Seek first the kingdom of God and His

righteousness, and all these things shall be added to you" (Matthew 6:33 NKJV).

3. There was an indifference to the world around them. Appeals to help the poor were seen as one more intrusion, one more effort to prop up those who could not manage their lives very well. As long as me and mine are all right, the rest of the world can go sailing by. The Laodiceans needed a vision for the world, beginning with the deplorable spiritual state of their own city and going from there to the world beyond.

4. They had settled for good enough. No one ever won the Olympics or excelled in any field at all who looked at natural talent or what he had in hand and decided it was good enough. The highest demands are required for the greatest results. The one who triumphs is the one who has been pushed, more by himself than others, to settle for nothing less than excellence. The Laodiceans had given something of themselves to the Lord, but not abandoned all of themselves before Him. They sought enough salvation to get them into Heaven but not enough to disturb the way they lived their lives. Francis Chan has noted, "Lukewarm people don't really want to be saved from their sin; they want only to be saved from the penalty of their sin."

They loved too little, gave too little, believed too little, settled for too little and so remained lame caricatures of true believers.

Sam Storms takes a different approach on this. " ...The word 'hot' refers to the well-known medicinal waters of Hierapolis where hot springs reached 95 degrees (35C). The word "cold," on the other hand, points to the refreshing waters of Colossae. The church was providing neither refreshment for the spiritually weary, portrayed through the image of cold water from Colossae ... nor healing for the spiritually sick, portrayed through the imagery of hot water from Hierapolis."[40]

No matter which interpretation is used, the church in Laodicea only excelled in disappointing Christ.

Spewing Them Out

The disgust that the Lord felt is explicitly pictured with the scene of Him spewing, or vomiting the Laodicean church out of His mouth. Of all the artist's renderings you will ever see of Christ, this is one no artist has sought to portray. It is horrifying to think of this from a Savior who came to seek and to save that which was lost, who reached the leper, the demoniac, the dying thief. To imagine that the sight of some in His church was causing this reaction is appalling.

Consider the image, as difficult as that might be. The ancient people used lukewarm salt water to induce vomiting. Given the condition of water in the city, such a scene was well known. The action of vomiting is hardly done in secret. Though a door is shut, the sound of retching betrays what is happening with the person. And the Lord's choice of this image means that the rejection of the lukewarm will not only be violent but obvious.

You say, 'I am rich; I have acquired wealth and do not need a thing.' But you do not realize that you are wretched, pitiful, poor, blind and naked. I counsel you to buy from me gold refined in the fire, so you can become rich; and white clothes to wear, so you can cover your shameful nakedness; and salve to put on your eyes, so you can see (Revelation 3:17-18).

Laodicea was known the world over for the wealth of the city, its thriving clothing industry, the production and sale of its eye medicine that gave such powerful relief. But though the city had these, spiritually the Laodicean church was on the opposite end of the spectrum.

---

[40]*Storms, 208-209*

LAODICEA: Lukewarm and Loving It

Three statements of Jesus define the church and its members.

1. **They thought they were rich but they were poor.** The booming banking, clothing and medicine industries supported hundreds of other businesses that supplied food, raw materials, tools and transport. Prosperity was making most everyone wealthy. Under those circumstances the Laodiceans may have felt that this must all have been God's blessing, a reward for their righteousness. The proof was in the pocketbook.

   But the Lord saw it differently. The money had not enriched them but impoverished them. Assuming the coins in their pocket meant that God blessed them, they did not examine their lives to see whether or not it was true. As in the days of the earthquake when the city had refused help from Rome, the Laodicean Christians saw themselves as doing just fine, in need of nothing. This spotlighted the most serious idol of all: the self.

   The truth was that they were far from being self-sufficient. Spiritually they had fallen to the worst state of poverty and deprivation. They were pathetic, like the homeless beggar whose presence on the street they despised.

   There is a story of Thomas Aquinas who saw a monk counting a large sum of money for the church. He said to the monk, "Well, my brother, no longer can the church say, 'Silver and gold have I none!'" "True," the monk answered, "nor can it say, 'In the name of Jesus Christ of Nazareth, rise and walk.'" While Judas sold his soul for 30 pieces of silver, the Laodicean church was like too many others who settled, sold Christ out for a much smaller sum.

2. **They thought they were richly clothed but they were naked.** The old children's story of "The Emperor's New Clothes" serves as a parable of the Laodicean church. Re-

call that a couple of conmen came to a kingdom governed by a very shallow and pretentious ruler. Assuring the emperor that they could make him a suit of clothing that only the wisest and most intelligent could see, they set about pretending to sew with thread that did not exist and cloth that appeared only in the imagination. They went through the formality of calling the emperor in for numerous fittings, all the time convincing him that only a fool could not see how beautiful the suit was. The emperor's staff, not wishing to appear foolish themselves, gushed about the exquisite workmanship and how stunning the emperor looked. Of course, neither the emperor nor anyone else could see anything but no one wanted

Hieropolis, the source of hot mineral springs for Laodicea. Cold springs were located in Colossae.

to admit him or herself a fool. It was decided that when the suit of imaginary clothing was finished, the emperor would parade through the town to show his people.

The word went out that only fools could not see the suit, the wise, on the other hand could fully comprehend its beauty. So the emperor sallied forth, completely naked, to parade in front of people whose pretensions were as bad as his. All the people praised the emperor and his suit, not only to flatter him but so they could appear wise in front of the others. All the while each wondered why he could see nothing. Finally, a little boy shouted out, "Look! The emperor is naked!" And so he was. All the pretensions in the world could not hide the nakedness of a pompous ruler.

The Laodiceans had the pretense of being clothed in stunning garments but Christ saw their hearts and they were naked. They might be able to fool one another, but the Lord was not taken in by the lies they told themselves.

3. They thought they could see but they were blind. They shipped their eye medicine far and wide. But in trying to cure the blindness of the world, they failed to perceive their own spiritual sightlessness. And like the blind, they were now in a place where someone else had to lead them because they could not find the way on their own anymore.

Their Only Hope

Counteracting this terrible condition the Lord counseled the Laodiceans to come to Him for what they needed. The words "from me" are emphatic, leaving no doubt that they are not to look anywhere else nor will they find what they need from anyone else but Him.

The Lord directed them to buy gold, which is like saying "Give me money for money." But in reality, it is their need, which is used to purchase the "gold" Christ is offering. In the end, the only thing they can offer the Lord is their need. It is the need presented by their blindness that is the reason the salve is applied. It is the need of their nakedness that initiates the offer of clothing. And not just any clothing but white raiment. The white symbolizes righteousness, the most pressing need of the Laodiceans (See also notes on Sardis.)

Despite their backsliding, the Lord stood before them to provide exactly what they needed at the point of their greatest need.

Those whom I love I rebuke and discipline. So be earnest and repent. Here I am! I stand at the door and knock. If anyone hears my voice and opens the door, I will come in and eat with that person, and they with me. To the one who is victorious, I will give the right to sit with me on my throne, just as I was victorious and sat down with my Father on His throne. Whoever has ears, let them hear what the Spirit says to the churches (Revelation 3:19-22).

After speaking to the Laodiceans in the harshest of terms and laying out for them in painstaking and unsparing detail the true condition that they are in, there is a softening tone of reconciliation. First, a word of explanation.

If the Laodiceans were not the objects of His love, He would not have been so angry with them. That love demands that action be taken in the form of rebukes and discipline. The word for rebuke involves showing a person what they have done wrong and calling them back from it. The term for discipline means to stir them up, to roust them to get their attention, which leads to corrective action.

It would not be thought unloving for a parent to sharply grab a child's arm who was stepping out into a busy street. A firm scolding would surely follow this action. Though the child might cry and complain that his arm aches, be saddened because his feelings were hurt, the loving thing is to act decisively and warn the child. Loving deeply means to rebuke when needed, to confront and to call the person back from a dangerous course. Indulging the wayward is not just lazy and self-protective; it shows contempt for the so-called object of love.

The response to that act of discipline should be to be earnest and repent. The word for earnest means to be "hot, zealous." Although the Laodiceans have been lukewarm up to this point, their repentance needs to be intense and done at full throttle. Here the offender is called, like the wayward prodigal son in the parable, from a life of feeding pigs in poverty, to once again enter the joyful father's presence.

At the Door

"Here I am! I stand at the door and knock ..."

According to Roman law, officials had the right to requisition lodging from any individual simply by demanding it. The owner could not refuse entry or lodging, even if it meant displacing family members to do so. Quite naturally, the officials did not choose to enter the poorest of homes but the ones that offered the most comfort. In a city like Laodicea where many were wealthy, the scene of a Roman official at the door was very familiar.

But contrasting the Roman demand is the striking humility of Christ. It was only a few lines back that He was rebuking the Laodiceans in the harshest tones with the most abrasive language. It would seem given that and the depth of their offenses, that He would have every right to pound on the door like one of the Roman officials, to demand entry and the best provision for Himself regardless of the discomfort it may cause. But no. There is no forced entry.

Ancient Bible commentator Oecumenius comments, "Here the Lord reveals His own humble and peaceful nature. The devil with axe and hammer smashes the doors of those who do not receive him ... but the Lord even now in the Song of Songs says to the bride, 'Open to me, my sister, my bride.'"[41]

So the choice is yours, dear Laodiceans. If you open, I will come in, Christ promised. Not to storm or rage against you but to share a quiet fellowship while enjoying a restored relationship. It is as if

---

[41] *Ancient Christian Commentary on Scripture, Volume XII, 55*

He is saying, "In allowing me to come into your house, you will find that you are the one who has come home."

Discussion Questions

1. What dangers are posed to the church when it is found in a luxurious setting?

2. When your church faces a problem, what are the steps taken to solve it? Where do prayer and waiting on God fall in the process?

3. Reread the conversation between Thomas Aquinas and the monk. What lesson is there for your church?

4. What would the Lord say to a church whose potlucks are well attended but whose prayer meetings and Bible studies languished?

5. How can the anger of Christ at the Laodiceans be reconciled with His humble request to come and dine with them?

Personal Reflection

1. Christ told the Laodiceans that He was the source of all creation. Since you are one of God's creations, reflect on what that says to you.

2. Describe the danger of spiritually settling for good enough.

3. The Laodiceans thought they were richly clothed but Christ saw them as shamefully naked. How can a person be so fooled at their state before the Lord?

4. Describe when the Lord used a need in your life to prove that He was the answer to it.

5. When is anger the proof of love?

CLOSING THOUGHTS

The words of Christ to the seven churches can be equally applied to individual Christians as well as congregations. What He says continues to challenge us to be shaken out of our complacency, while on the other hand to feel His embrace when we are wounded in the fight.

There are several themes that consistently are presented in these seven letters.

1. Although Christ's salvation is open to all in whatever condition they might be, once a person is saved the Lord expects the believer to be and act differently. The Ephesian church was commanded to repent and find again its first love. Sardis was told that in spite of its bloated self-image, it was incomplete. Those churches that had strayed were not told to settle in but to fall back into line.

   In the present day there is a misty idea of God that pictures Him as a coddling, somewhat needy deity that chuckles away the transgressions of His misbehaving children. Even worse, God is seen as someone who whisks away any and all to Glory despite the life they have lived or the ways a person has disregarded Him. Just as often, those who seek to follow Him are pictured as dull and self-righteous, despisers of beauty and joy as opposed to the fun-loving free spirits who live life to the fullest. While Hollywood has crafted a theology of such a two-dimensional divinity with automaton followers, there is not even the hint of an anemic Almighty or of plastic disciples presented in Revelation.

   Presented instead is the Christ who stands in strength, and whose authority is so irresistible that no one who opposes Him can stand. Exercising that authority, and knowing the full extent of the salvation that He has offered, He defines what He meant during His earthly ministry when He said, "Whoever wants to be my disciple must deny themselves and take up their cross and follow me" (Matthew 16:24). This is not a multiple choice Christianity but a one-way road of holy obedience. Because Christ empowers His child the expectation is that the believer will then so live. And rather than meekly indulging the disobedient, God stands as the judge who demands accountability.

2. The life in Christ is to be boldly lived regardless of the surroundings where the person finds himself. The seven churches were located in both large and small towns, wealthy and poor settings, among the refined and the crude. Regardless of what the place looked like or its most outstanding feature, each offered its own challenges to the Christian faith. Pergamum was the place of Satan's throne. Smyrna's atmosphere was so toxic that the Lord could only promise the church further persecution. While Christ readily acknowledged that because of that there were unique difficulties that had to be met, the life found in Him was dynamic enough to not only meet those problems but also overcome them. One of the testimonies of Scripture is that there are no perfect places of service. Despite Adam and Eve being placed in a perfect environment, sin entered. On the other hand, regardless of the wickedness in a place the power of God exceeds the power of evil.

3. Our allegiance to Christ is to define our relationships with others. It was the misguided deference to the woman called Jezebel in Thyatira that brought condemnation from Christ. The tolerance of the Nicolaitans proved a deadly danger to the church in Pergamum with a similar problem in Thyatira. Because the people of God belong to Him, of necessity there is an estrangement from those who stand against the Lord. Jesus warned, "Do not sup-

pose that I have come to bring peace to the earth. I did not come to bring peace, but a sword" (Matthew 10:34).

This seems to create a tension. Believers are unavoidably placed in a world that is hostile to Christ as surely as a ship is placed in the very sea that would sink it. Beyond that, there is no way to win people to Christ without coming up close to those who are lost.

But if we look closely at what Christ says to the churches we quickly realize that He is not urging believers to cut themselves off from unbelievers. Instead, He is warning against those who label themselves as Christians but whose lifestyle and testimony reveal they are wolves in sheep's clothing. The contrast between believers and pretenders is not always as easy to spot as it might seem. Again, the gospels give us an illustration of this in the parable of the wheat and the tares (Matthew 13:24-30).

The disciple of Christ must be discerning, seeking the guidance of the Holy Spirit. If he realizes that there is someone who is leading a false life while maintaining that his or her life and witness is sound, the believer has the obligation to deal with the other person. If that person refuses to acknowledge wrongdoing as Jezebel did in Thyatira, the believer has no choice but to distance himself from the person to avoid the risk of spiritual ruin. The pull of gravity downward is greater than the lift of bird's wings upwards. As Paul solemnly warns, "If you think you are standing firm, be careful that you don't fall" (1 Corinthians 10:12). When allegiance to Christ is replaced by loyalty to His enemies, disaster is inevitable.

4. Our relationship with Christ defines our worldview. The world was not a friendly place for the believer in any of the cities. Both Philadelphia and Smyrna were enduring an onslaught of persecution. Ephesus, Thyatira and Pergamum were battling the insidious seduction of those within the

church. Laodicea faced the worse reaction to its presence of all: indifference.

Even though the struggles were bitter, in none of the circumstances faced by the churches does Christ order a retreat. The Christian is to take his stand in a world, a hostile world, as a witness for Christ. The worldview of the believer is one that recognizes that the world is fallen and as such is broken and scarred. Sin has so distorted people that even when they know something is wrong, they often resist the only hope to correct it. Fortunately, the Holy Spirit continually outflanks the enemy so that people have an opportunity to respond. But even with that, the world remains at war against God. Christianity has been, must be countercultural. James declared the truth bluntly, "You adulterous people, don't you know that friendship with the world means enmity against God? Therefore, anyone who chooses to be a friend of the world becomes an enemy of God" (James 4:4).

We engage the world to transform it, not to appease it.

5. The follower of Christ will be rewarded for his faithfulness. The Ephesian faithful were promised they would eat from the tree of life. The loyal ones in Smyrna were promised the crown of life. Pergamum believers could look forward to a new name while the faithful in Thyatira were pledged the morning star. Lovers of the Lord in Sardis were told that their names would be in the Book of Life. The stalwarts in Philadelphia could look forward to being recognized as pillars in the Temple of God. And even the wayward Laodiceans were told that the Savior of the ages would sit down and dine with them. None of these promises were intended only for the church to which they were addressed but to faithful believers in all places at all times. By putting the promises together we are given a beautiful composite picture of how Christ intends to lovingly wel-

come home His devoted warriors.

John no doubt would see the parallel between what happened in Christ's earthly life and how the Christ life was lived in the believer. His Lord had suffered cruelly and unspeakably but all of that was swallowed up at the moment of resurrection. It wasn't the beaten and bruised Christ that John now followed, but the risen, glorious, all-powerful Lord of the ages. And this victorious Lord comforts His suffering church, His vexed and tormented followers with the promise that not only will the affliction cease, it will be replaced with indescribable glory. When writing to his fellow believers, the Apostle John expressed it, "Dear friends, now we are children of God, and what we will be has not yet been made known. But we know that when Christ appears, we shall be like Him, for we shall see Him as He is" (1 John 3:2). There is no more blessed hope.

Bibliography

Barclay, William. *Letters to the Seven Churches*, Abingdon Press: Nashville, 1957

Daniels, T. Scott. *Seven Deadly Spirits*, Baker Academic: Grand Rapids, 2009

Earle, Ralph. *Beacon Bible Commentary: Hebrews to Revelation* Volume 10, Beacon Hill Press: Kansas City, 1967

Eckley, Richard K. Revelation: *A Commentary for Bible Students*, Wesleyan Publishing House: Indianapolis, 2006

Evans, William. *Christ's Last Message to the Church*, Fleming H. Revell Company: New York, 1926

Fadiman, Clifton and Bernard, Andre. *Bartlett's Book of Anecdotes*, Little, Brown and Company: Boston, 2000

Groseclose, Win. *Letters to the Seven Churches*, 2006

Hemer, Colin J. *The Letters to the Seven Churches in Asia*, William B. Eerdmans Publishing Company: Grand Rapids, 1989

Jones, William H. *Seven Churches and Their Report Cards*, ChiRho Communications, 2011

Kelshaw, Terence. *Dangerous Liaisons: Seven Churches in Revelation*, Rio Grande Monograph, 1996

Oxford Dictionary of Quotations, Oxford University Press: New York, 1980

Ramsey, Sir William. *The Letters to the Seven Churches,* Kessinger Publishing: Whitefish, Montana, 2004

Rotz, Carol. *Revelation: A Commentary in the Wesleyan Tradition,* Beacon Hill Press: Kansas City, 2012

Storms, Sam. *To the One Who Conquers: 50 Daily Meditations on the Seven Letters of Revelation 2-3,* Crossway Books: Wheaton, IL, 2008

Stott, John. *What Christ Thinks of the Church,* Monarch Books: London, 2003

Ulery, Kent. *No Longer at Ease: Seven Churches and the Empire, a Study in Revelation 1-3,* 2011

Weinrich, William C. (Editor). *Ancient Christian Commentary on Scripture: Revelation Volume 12,* Intervarsity Press: Downer's Grove, IL, 2005

Wells, Albert M. Jr. *Inspiring Quotations Contemporary and Classic,* Thomas Nelson Publishers: Nashville, 1988

White, Malcolm. *You've Got Mail,* Two Edged Sword Publications: Waterlooville, Hampshire, UK, 2007

CREST **BOOKS**

Salvation Army National Headquarters
Alexandria, VA, USA

Crest Books, a division of The Salvation Army's National Publications Department, was established in 1997 so contemporary Salvationist voices could be captured and bound in enduring form for future generations, to serve as witnesses to the continuing force and mission of the Army.

Stephen Banfield and Donna Leedom, *Say Something*

Judith L. Brown and Christine Poff, eds., *No Longer Missing: Compelling True Stories from The Salvation Army's Missing Persons Ministry*

Terry Camsey, *Slightly Off Center! Growth Principles to Thaw Frozen Paradigms*

Marlene Chase, *Pictures from the Word; Beside Still Waters: Great Prayers of the Bible for Today; Our God Comes: And Will Not Be Silent*

John Cheydleur and Ed Forster, eds., *Every Sober Day Is a Miracle*

Helen Clifton, From Her Heart: *Selections from the Preaching and Teaching of Helen Clifton*

Shaw Clifton, *Never the Same Again: Encouragement for New and Not–So–New Christians; Who Are These Salvationists? An Analysis for the 21st Century; Selected Writings, Vol. 1: 1974-1999 and Vol. 2: 2000-2010*

Christmas Through the Years: A War Cry Treasury

Frank Duracher, *Smoky Mountain High*

Easter Through the Years: A War Cry Treasury

Ken Elliott, *The Girl Who Invaded America: The Odyssey Of Eliza Shirley*
Ed Forster, *101 Everyday Sayings From the Bible*

William Francis, *Celebrate the Feasts of the Lord: The Christian Heritage of the Sacred Jewish Festivals*

Henry Gariepy, *Israel L. Gaither: Man with a Mission; A Salvationist Treasury: 365 Devotional Meditations from the Classics to the Contemporary; Andy Miller: A Legend and a Legacy*

Henry Gariepy and Stephen Court, *Hallmarks of The Salvation Army*

Roger J. Green, *The Life and Ministry of William Booth* (with Abingdon Press, Nashville)

How I Met The Salvation Army

Carroll Ferguson Hunt, *If Two Shall Agree* (with Beacon Hill Press, Kansas City)

John C. Izzard, *Pen of Flame: The Life and Poetry of Catherine Baird*

David Laeger, *Shadow and Substance: The Tabernacle of the Human Heart*

John Larsson, *Saying Yes to Life*

Living Portraits Speaking Still: A Collection of Bible Studies

Herbert Luhn, *Holy Living: The Mindset of Jesus*

Philip Needham, *He Who Laughed First: Delighting in a Holy God,* (with Beacon Hill Press, Kansas City)

R.G. Moyles, *I Knew William Booth; Come Join Our Army; William Booth in America: Six Visits 1886 - 1907; Farewell to the Founder*

Joe Noland, *A Little Greatness*

Quotes of the Past & Present

Lyell M. Rader, *Romance and Dynamite: Essays on Science and the Nature of Faith*

R. David Rightmire, *Sanctified Sanity: The Life and Teaching of Samuel Logan Brengle*

Allen Satterlee, *Determined to Conquer: The History of The Salvation Army Caribbean Territory; Voices from Haiti; Salvation Assault: The History of The Salvation Army in Papua New Guinea; Turning Points: How The Salvation Army Found a Different Path; Sweeping Through the Land: The History of The Salvation Army in the Southern United States; Notable Quotables: A Compendium of Gems from Salvation Army Literature*

Harry Williams, *An Army Needs An Ambulance Corps: A History of The Salvation Army's Medical Services*

A. Kenneth Wilson, *Fractured Parables: And Other Tales to Lighten the Heart and Quicken the Spirit; The First Dysfunctional Family: A Modern Guide to the Book of Genesis, It Seemed Like a Good Idea at the Time: Some of the Best and Worst Decisions in the Bible*

A Word in Season: A Collection of Short Stories

Check Yee, *Good Morning China*

Chick Yuill, *Leadership on the Axis of Change*